Busy with Bugs

160 Extremely Interesting Things to Do with Bugs

Toni Albert

Illustrated by Margaret Brandt

Have fun with BUGS!

Toni Albert

Trickle Creek Books
500 Andersontown Road
Mechanicsburg, PA 17055

www.TrickleCreekBooks.com

Dedication

For children who love animals, even the little animals we call BUGS. For the children in my life: Avery, Sawyer, Evan, and Ellie. For Bob, of course.

• • • • • • • • • • • • •

Library of Congress Control Number: 2010920941
Publisher's Cataloging-in-Publication
(Provided by Quality Books, Inc.)

Albert, Toni.
    Busy with bugs : 160 extremely interesting things to do with bugs / Toni Albert ; illustrated by Margaret Brandt. — 1st ed.
    p. cm.
    SUMMARY: A guide for exploring the miniature world of insects that live in a child's own backyard, including bug anatomy, behavior, life cycle and habitat.
    Audience: Grades 3-8.
    Includes bibliographical references and index.
    ISBN-13: 978-1-929432-05-9
    ISBN-10: 1-929432-05-4
    ISBN-13: 978-1-929432-06-6
    ISBN-10: 1-929432-06-2

    1. Insects—Juvenile literature. 2. Insects—North America—Juvenile literature. [1. Insects.] I. Brandt, Margaret, ill. II. Title.

QL467.2.A43 2010   595.7
                    QBI10-600013

Published in the United States by Trickle Creek Books, 500 Andersontown Road, Mechanicsburg, PA 17055.

Cover design by Robert and Toni Albert, illustrations by Margaret Brandt.

• • • • • • • • • • • • •

Note to Readers

The publisher has endeavored to ensure that the experiments and activities in this book are safe, but we assume no responsibility for any accident, injury, loss, or damage arising from any of the activities. Children should be supervised when they try the activities.

CPSIA tracking label information:

Nansha, Guangdong, China
Date of Production: 05/2010
Cohort: Batch 1

Trickle Creek Books

Field Notes

• • • • • • • • • • • •

Bug Sizer

1   2   3   4   5   6

Date _____

Time of day _____

Weather conditions _____

Location • (City and state) _____

Description of the exact place where you found the bug • (Example: Under a rock.)

_____

_____

Description of the bug _____

_____

_____

Interesting observations • (Example: Caterpillar was eating maple leaves.)

_____

_____

Sketch of bug

Name of bug • (Use a field guide to identify bug.) _____

Contents

• • • • • • • • • • • •

Trickle Creek Books

Introduction

I really like bugs. I like their names — Ferocious Water Bug, Jagged Assassin Bug, Golden-Orange Bumble Bee, Striped Cucumber Beetle, Secret Cave Cricket, and Eastern Toe-Biter. I love their colors and patterns, especially the bright stripes and dots on many beetles, the brilliant blues and greens of dragonflies, and of course, the hand-painted wings of butterflies. I enjoy the soft, prickly feel of a Wooly Bear Caterpillar in my hand. I'm utterly amazed when I watch ants work together or taste sweet honey made by bees or listen to bug song on a late summer evening.

As I wrote this book, I was reminded that bugs are little animals. Getting to know them helps us understand the entire Animal Kingdom. Bugs live in every kind of habitat: mountains, deserts, rainforests, caves, rivers, oceans, fields, backyards — and our houses. Some bugs are predators; some are prey. Some are diurnal (active during the day); some are nocturnal (active at night). Some bugs hibernate; some migrate. Bugs fly, hop, crawl, and run. They eat, drink, rest, hide, communicate, build homes, raise young, attack, fight, die. They are little animals.

And since bugs are animals, we must treat them with respect and care. I know what you're thinking. No one welcomes Japanese Beetles in the garden. We don't want to be kind to mosquitoes. And absolutely no one wants a pet tick. But this book is packed with interesting activities, including collecting and keeping live bugs. By handling them gently and taking care of them responsibly, you'll learn to love and protect all living things on our planet. You'll become a better caretaker of our earth.

Bug Giggle • Giggle when you read this.

If you don't know the meaning of a word, check the glossary on pages 62 and 63.

Name of Bug

Note: Many kinds of bugs are found all over the world, but this book only gives information about where bugs are found in the United States.

Activities • Experiment, explore, discover, have fun, be careful.

Field Guide • To collect bugs, find out what to look for and when and where to look.

Bug Buzz • Read, open your eyes wide, and let your jaw drop. Be amazed!

Bugs and the Environment

• • • • • • • • • • • • • • •

Have you ever spread a picnic on the ground and then wondered how so many bugs could suddenly find you? Our world is filled with insects and bugs. More than a million species of insects alone have been described and classified. Scientists believe there are millions more. If you spent your entire life counting bugs on earth, you wouldn't have time to finish. You would have to count a billion billion bugs.

All living things are important to our environment, but partly because of their great numbers, bugs are especially important. Some tiny bugs are big troublemakers that spread diseases and wipe out crops. But other bugs are essential for life on earth. Bugs are food for many animals, including birds, bats, lizards, frogs, and fish. Some bugs are decomposers, which clean up everything from dead leaves to dead bodies. Others, especially certain flies, bees, and wasps, are pollinators. They carry pollen from flower to flower, enabling trees to bear fruit and flowers to make more flowers. Bugs also help keep nature in balance. They keep "invader plants" and insect pests under control by eating them.

If bugs were to disappear, it would affect our entire planet. And bugs *are* disappearing. Like all animals, they are harmed by polluted air, water, and soil. They become endangered or extinct when they lose their habitats. Three-quarters of all the animal species in tropical rainforests are insects. Scientists are scrambling to name and count new bugs before the rainforests are completely destroyed.

What can we do to help protect our favorite bugs?

- Do everything you can to take care of our earth. Recycle, turn off lights, don't waste water, etc. (You know what to do!)

- Don't use pesticides. They kill good bugs as well as bad ones.

- Don't buy mounted butterflies or beetles collected in rainforests.

- Plant a butterfly garden — or a caterpillar garden. Any kind of garden will be a habitat for bugs.

• • • • • • • • • • • • • •

What are bugs?

Children think of bugs as little crawly creatures, which may or may not be insects. All insects have six legs. Included in this book are spiders, which are not insects because they have eight legs; millipedes, which have dozens of legs; and pill bugs, which are really crustaceans like shrimp. But insect scientists (entomologists) only use the word *bugs* to refer to insects in a group called Hemiptera. These are true bugs. Almost all true bugs have beak-like mouth parts and front wings that fold flat over their backs. Water striders, bed bugs, and assassin bugs are true bugs.

7

Collecting Bugs

To become a great bug collector, begin by noticing bugs. Look closely at a bug — and more and more closely. What is the bug doing? Where does it hide? What color is it? How big is it? Use a field guide with photographs of insects and spiders to identify the bug.

As you teach yourself how to find bugs, you will soon learn that each bug lives in a particular habitat, the place that is exactly right for it. A bug's habitat provides the perfect food, water, and shelter for it. A dragonfly's habitat is a pond or stream. A millipede's habitat is damp leaf litter. Caterpillars are found on trees and shrubs. Grasshoppers are found in grass (of course). Once you know a bug's habitat, you'll know where to look for that bug.

A good place to look for bugs is under a large rock or rotting log. You may find millipedes, centipedes, ants, beetles, snails, slugs, worms, crickets, spiders, or pill bugs there. Use a paintbrush to push any interesting bugs into your collecting jar. Then gently replace the rock or log in its original position.

Beat Sheet

Fly-Right-In Bug Trap

Please-Drop-In Bug Trap

Creep-Under Bug Trap

Insect Net

Camera

Damp paper towel to keep bugs from losing moisture and to give them a place to hide

Small paintbrush for pushing insects into the jar

6-inch Ruler

Jar and lid with small holes in it

Pocket Field Guide to Insects

Magnifying Lens

Day Pack

Pencil and colored pencils for notes and sketches

Notebook

Catch a Bug

1 Make a Bug Kit to take with you when you go bug hunting. Look at the illustration on this page for ideas of what you might include in your kit.

2 Make a Beat Sheet by putting a heavy white cloth under a tree or shrub. Beat or shake the branches. Did any bugs fall on the sheet? Scoop them up into your collecting jar.

3 Use an insect net to catch bugs in high grass or weeds. Quickly sweep the net back and forth. When you catch something, turn the handle a half turn, so the net is folded over at the top, trapping the bugs inside. Hold the bottom of the net up high until the bugs climb upward, and grasp the net with your hand to keep them there. Then turn the net inside out over your jar, dump the bugs inside, and don't forget the lid!

4 Make a Please-Drop-In Bug Trap. Dig a hole in the ground and put a plastic container in it with the top of the container level with the ground. Put four large stones on the ground around the mouth of the container and balance a piece of wood on the stones to keep rain out. Check the trap every day and record which bugs you find. Then release them.

5 Make a Creep-Under Bug Trap by spreading a thick mat of grass clippings on the ground. Lay a black plastic garbage bag or a piece of wood on top of the grass. After a week, lift the trap carefully and see who moved in.

6 Make a Fly-Right-In Bug Trap to catch flying bugs. Put bits of fruit in a wide-mouth jar, or at night, put a glow stick in a jar to catch bugs that are attracted to light. Place a funnel in the jar with the small end of the funnel pointing down. Then when bugs fly in, they won't be able to get out again. Observe them carefully, then release them.

Trickle Creek Books

Keeping Bugs

The most interesting way to study bugs is to keep one — or more — as a pet. But remember that bugs are little animals and they must be cared for properly. You can collect bugs outside or you can buy them at a pet store or from a biological supply company. Find out the name of your bug, its natural habitat, and its diet. It will be your job to provide a home for the bug as much like its home in nature as you can.

Make sure your bug has water from the moment you collect it. A damp, crumpled paper towel in the collecting jar will provide both water and shelter. Later, when your bug is in its new home, you can keep a damp cotton ball in its cage or you can spray a fine mist of water in the cage. A bug needs water every day just like you do.

If you keep your bug long enough, you may be able to watch its entire life cycle. Or you might want to observe the bug for only a few days and then release it. If you can't find the right food for a bug and you don't see it eating what you offer, let it go.

Daddy Longlegs, Millipedes, and Pill Bugs in a Terrarium

Food ● Bits of fruits and vegetables, decaying leaf litter, oak leaves for millipedes
Water ● Damp paper towel
Shelter ● Layer of dirt, leaf litter, damp piece of bark

Cicadas in a Jar

Food ● Adults don't eat, but they suck sap from leaves
Water ● Damp paper towel
Shelter ● Layer of dirt, sticks to climb on

Whirligig Beetles in an Aquarium

Food ● Water insects, dead insects, sliver of cooked meat
Water ● Pond water
Shelter ● Twig to climb up out of water

Ladybird Beetles in a Bug Cage

Food ● Aphids or softened raisins
Water ● Damp paper towel
Shelter ● Leaves

Bug Habitats

Grasshoppers in a Mesh Tent

Food ● Grass, leafy vegetables
Water ● Mist from spray bottle
Shelter ● Layer of dirt; leafy branches to climb on

Every bug needs the right food, water, and shelter.
See pages 64 and 65 for the information you need
to keep the bugs featured in this book.

How to Keep Bugs

Keeping a bug in a cage is just like taking care of a pet. You need to give it exactly the right food, water, and shelter to keep it alive. And each kind of bug has different needs.

See if your butterfly will feed from fresh flowers before you let it go.

Butterfly House

Butterflies in a Butterfly House
Food • Fresh-cut nectar flowers
Water • Mist from spray bottle

Keep a Bug

7 Find an interesting bug to keep as a pet. Can you make it feel at home? Choose a roomy container — a plastic jar, a terrarium, or a bug cage you buy. Use a piece of fabric secured with a rubber band to make an escape-proof lid that will allow plenty of air into the cage. Find out all you can about your bug. Give your bug water, shelter, and its favorite food.

8 Keep a Bug Book — a Click Beetle Chronicle, an Ant Account, or a Millipede Memoir. Watch your bug each day and record what you see. Measure it. Make sketches or take photos. Make up a cartoon or a story about your bug. Fill your book with information that you learn about the bug. Make the best bug book ever.

9 If you find insect eggs, a cocoon, a chrysalis, or a pupa attached to a limb or stalk, don't try to take them inside. Just attach a fine mesh bag over the entire limb. Then check it often. Who knows what you might see!

10 Make a butterfly house with two large embroidery hoops and one yard of fine netting. To find the circumference of the embroidery hoop, pull a tape measure around the outside of the hoop. Cut the netting so the width is one and one-half times the circumference of the hoop and the length is one yard long. Shape the netting into a tube that is one yard long with the same circumference as the hoop. Part of the tube will have a double layer of netting. Slip the smaller part of the embroidery hoop inside the tube of netting and fasten the larger part of the hoop over the smaller on the outside. Leave enough netting above the hoop to secure it with string. Finish the other end of the tube the same way. Catch a butterfly with cupped hands. Don't touch its wings. Find the opening in the side of the netting, Slip your hand in, and release the butterfly.

11

Anatomy of Insects

· · · · · · · · · · · · · · · ·

Anatomy: *The study of the form or structure of animals or plants; looking at the different parts of an animal or plant.*

There are more than a million kinds of insects in the world — all different shapes and sizes and colors. How can you know that two little animals as different as a butterfly and a praying mantis are both insects? What do they have in common? We identify insects by looking at the parts of their bodies. All insects have three major body sections (head, thorax, and abdomen), six legs, and two antennae.

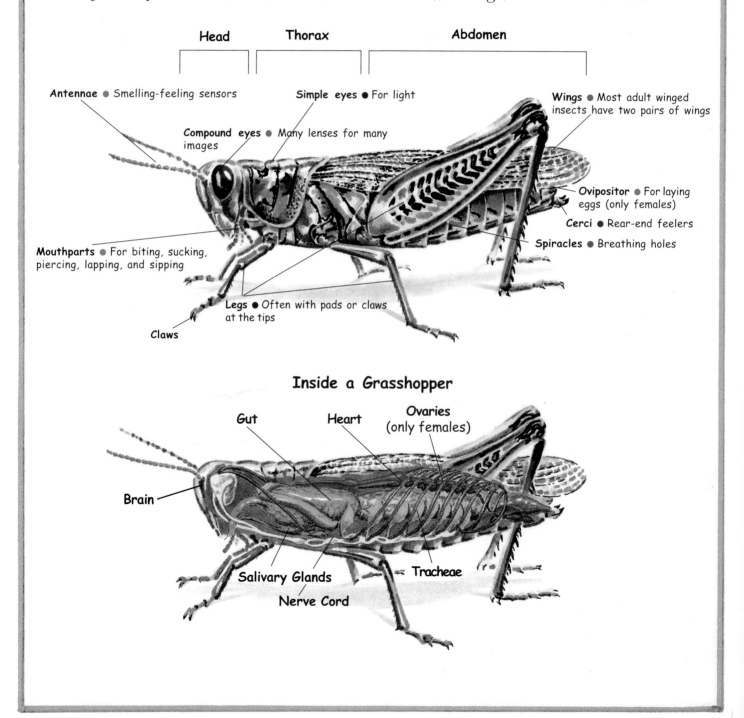

Head   Thorax   Abdomen

Antennae ● Smelling-feeling sensors

Simple eyes ● For light

Compound eyes ● Many lenses for many images

Wings ● Most adult winged insects have two pairs of wings

Ovipositor ● For laying eggs (only females)

Cerci ● Rear-end feelers

Spiracles ● Breathing holes

Mouthparts ● For biting, sucking, piercing, lapping, and sipping

Legs ● Often with pads or claws at the tips

Claws

Inside a Grasshopper

Gut   Heart   Ovaries (only females)

Brain

Salivary Glands

Nerve Cord

Tracheae

Classification of Insects

To keep track of all the animals on earth, scientists have classified them, or divided them into groups. The largest group is called a kingdom. The animal kingdom contains all animals, including all bugs and including you.

By carefully considering the anatomy of every animal, scientists have divided them into smaller and smaller groups. First the animal kingdom is divided into phyla; then each phylum is divided into classes; each class is divided into orders; each order is divided into families; each family is divided into genera; each genus is divided into species.

When you think of a certain kind of insect, you are probably thinking of a species, such as the Honey Bee. There are more than a million species of insects in the world.

Classification of the Honey Bee

Kingdom	Animal
Phylum	Arthropoda
Class	Insecta
Order	Hymenoptera
Family	Apidae
Genus	*Apis*
Species	*mellifera*

The bee's common name is Honey Bee. Its scientific name includes the genus and species: *Apis mellifera.*

Look at a Bug

11 All insects have six legs. Is a spider an insect? Is a millipede? Is a pill bug? Is a daddy longlegs? Find a bug and count its legs. Then you'll know right away if it's an insect.

12 Catch a bug and put it in a bug jar. Spend some time looking and looking at the bug. Can you see its antennae? Do they move? Look at its legs. Do they bend and have joints? Are there claws on its feet? Look at the eyes. How many are there? Look for wings. Look for feelers at the tip of its abdomen. Look at its mouthparts.

13 Make a sketch of your bug and try to label as many of its parts as you can: the head, eyes, mouthparts, antennae, thorax, legs, wings, abdomen, and feelers (cerci).

14 Catch a different kind of bug. Look at it carefully, sketch it, label its parts. What are the biggest differences between your two bugs?

15 The best way to really examine a bug is with a magnifying lens. You may be amazed to see big compound bug eyes or beautiful patterns of line and color. A typical magnifying glass has a magnifying power of 2X to 8X, but if you have a lens or loupe with a power of 20X or more, you'll find it very exciting.

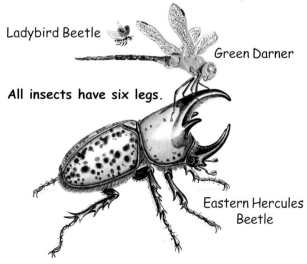

Ladybird Beetle

Green Darner

All insects have six legs.

Eastern Hercules Beetle

Trickle Creek Books

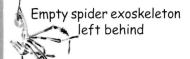
Empty spider exoskeleton
left behind

How Bugs Grow

. . . .

You and I have a skeleton made up of bones inside our bodies. Insects and spiders have skeletons, too, but theirs are outer skeletons, or exoskeletons. A bug's exoskeleton is a hard outer covering that cannot stretch, so as the bug grows, it wiggles out of its tight exoskeleton and forms a new one. A bug sheds, or molts, its exoskeleton several times as it grows bigger and bigger.

Many insects pass through four stages of growth: egg, larva, pupa, and adult. The larva is the active stage when the insect is eating and growing. The larva looks very different from the adult. The pupa is a resting stage while the insect is transforming into an adult. This kind of growth is called complete metamorphosis. Butterflies, moths, flies, beetles, wasps, and bees grow this way.

Other insects, such as grasshoppers, mantises, true bugs, and crickets don't have a pupa stage, so their growth is called incomplete metamorphosis. They are not transformed into something new like a caterpillar becoming a butterfly. The young, which are called nymphs, look like small adults. For example, a baby grasshopper looks like a tiny adult grasshopper. It grows by molting a number of times.

Metamorphosis is a change in form as an insect grows.

Flour Beetle
Eggs

Larva (grub) • Active, feeding stage

Larvae grow by molting several times.

Pupa • Resting stage while young insect turns into adult

Flour Beetles grow by complete metamorphosis.

Adult Flour Beetle

. . . .

Grasshopper
Eggs

Nymph hatching

Nymph looks like a little adult

Nymph molting

Insects and spiders molt by shedding their skins.

Grasshoppers grow by incomplete metamorphosis.

Spiders molt even after becoming adults.

Adult Grasshopper

A gall is a plant growth used as a home by insects.

Larva inside its gall house

The gall provides both food and shelter for the larva.

Look for oak apple galls on oak leaves or under oak trees.

Common Spangle Galls

Galls make an interesting collection because they are so varied. They may be soft or woody, pointed or round, smooth or hairy.

Look for moss galls on wild roses.

Look for goldenrod galls on the stems of goldenrod flowers.

Bug Shapes

16 When you find a dead insect, look at it carefully. If it appears hollow and has a slit or hole in it, it may not be a bug at all. It may be an exoskeleton that was shed and left behind as an insect grew. You can make a collection of exoskeletons. They are sometimes perfect in every detail, even including antennae, eye coverings, and legs.

17 Buy ten small crickets from a pet store, the smallest crickets you see. Keep the crickets as pets. (*See page 23 for directions.*) As your crickets grow, watch for signs of molting. Look for shed exoskeletons, which are split in half. You may even see a soft, rubbery cricket that hasn't yet formed its new hard exoskeleton.

18 One of the most magical changes in all of nature is the transformation of a caterpillar into a butterfly. (*See page 41 for directions on how to raise a caterpillar and watch its metamorphosis into a butterfly.*) Enjoy!

19 Some wasps, flies, and beetles are gall-makers. When they lay their eggs on a particular plant, they give off chemicals that make the plant produce a gall, which becomes a home for the insect larvae. Inside the gall, the larvae feed on plant juices and change into adults. Look for unusual plant growths that may be galls and make a collection.

20 If the gall has little holes in it, the insects inside it may have bored their way out. With an adult's help, cut the gall in half to see the rooms inside and the passages leading out. Can you tell how many insects were in it?

21 If you have a gall without holes, keep it in a cool place in a jar with a lid. Something will hatch, but you never know what! Besides the gall-maker's larvae, there may be uninvited guests that moved into the gall to find shelter or to eat the larvae.

Trickle Creek Books

Mimicry and Camouflage

Bugs get eaten a lot. All kinds of animals — from birds to fish, from frogs to monkeys — find them delicious. But bugs have many ways of hiding from predators, including the amazing ability to disguise themselves. Some bugs, like green grasshoppers in green grass, camouflage themselves by vanishing into their surroundings. Other bugs, like moths that look like wasps, mimic bugs and other animals that are poisonous or dangerous.

Camouflage often includes both color and shape. A katydid is not only green like a leaf but its wings are shaped like leaves. A walkingstick is brown like a stick and it is shaped like a stick. Camouflage may also include the way a bug acts. Some bugs that rely on camouflage for protection position themselves just right so that no one can see them. Some predator insects, like praying mantises, use camouflage for surprise attacks.

Insect mimics are some of the most incredible and interesting insects on earth. Think of a praying mantis that looks like an orchid or a treehopper that resembles a thorn. Or how about a caterpillar that looks like bird poop? It seems that insects will do anything to stay safe!

Camouflage ● A Giant Walkingstick is the color and shape of a stick and it positions itself like the twigs around it.

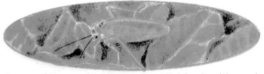

Camouflage ● A True Katydid looks like a leaf, is shaped like a leaf, and "hangs" like a leaf.

How can you tell that this insect is really a moth? (Its antennae are not bent like those of a wasp and it doesn't have a thin waist like a wasp.)

Mimicry ● A harmless Black-banded Wasp Moth looks like a wasp and acts like a wasp. It holds its wings the way a wasp does and can curve its body like a wasp about to sting.

Many bugs use camouflage for protection, but the White Orchid Mantid disguises itself as a flower to fool its prey.

Thorn-mimic Treehoppers look like thorns.

No animal wants to eat a Swallowtail Caterpillar. It looks like bird poop. How clever is that?

Tulip Tree Beauty

Big Poplar Sphinx

Sweetheart Underwing

Can you find three moths on these tree trunks?

Is it easier to see a butterfly in flight or when it's resting?

Grey Comma

Long-tailed Skipper

Bug Disguises

22 Think of an interesting place: a desert, a rainforest, a snow covered field, a city in China. Imagine yourself trying to hide in that place by using camouflage. How would you change your appearance? How would you act?

23 Most moths are active at night. During the day, they rest on tree trunks or vegetation and rely on camouflage for protection. Try to find a resting moth by looking closely at the trunks of trees. You may find a moth clinging to the tree, resting under loose bark, or hiding in a small opening in the tree trunk. Look closely because the moth may look just like the tree bark.

24 Watch a butterfly for as long as you can. Is it easier to see the butterfly when it flies or when it lands? Many butterflies show the bright colors on top of their wings while they are moving, but when they fold their wings to rest, the under surfaces of the wings are darker and provide good camouflage.

25 Try this experiment with some friends. Cut pieces of green, white, yellow, and blue construction paper into 1/2-inch pieces. Give each person twenty pieces of each color. Assign each person a small area outside where the grass is green. Then have each one toss his or her scraps of paper into the grass. Give yourselves 30 seconds to pick up as many pieces of paper as possible. The only rule is that you can't scoop up the paper scraps; you must pick them up one piece at a time. Then count the pieces you picked up, separating them by color. Did anyone pick up all twenty of the green scraps? Was it easier to find the other colors? Which color was easiest to locate?

Green Darner

Twelve-spot Skimmer

Dragonflies

Dragonflies
(Class Insecta, Order Odonata)

Look for: A large slender insect (from ¾"- 5" long) with huge compound eyes and two sets of transparent wings with delicate veins. Their bodies are often shiny, iridescent colors.

Where to look: Near water, especially ponds, lakes, and streams.

When to look: Spring, summer, fall.

Range: Throughout the United States.

Bug Giggle
Why did the prince think the princess was crazy? She said she saw a dragon fly over the pond.

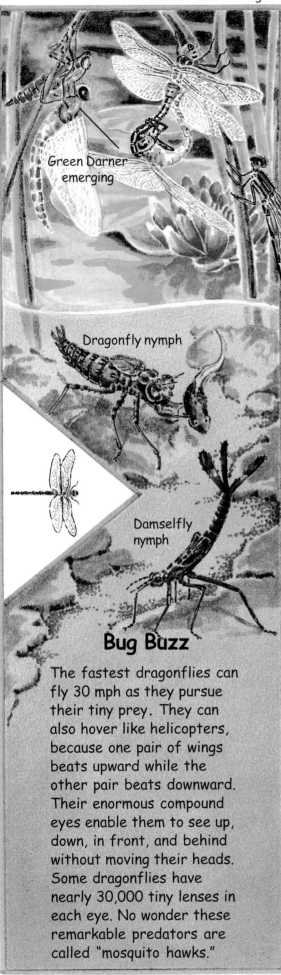

Green Darners mating

Green Darner emerging

Violet Tail Damselfly

Dragonfly nymph

Damselfly nymph

Bug Buzz

The fastest dragonflies can fly 30 mph as they pursue their tiny prey. They can also hover like helicopters, because one pair of wings beats upward while the other pair beats downward. Their enormous compound eyes enable them to see up, down, in front, and behind without moving their heads. Some dragonflies have nearly 30,000 tiny lenses in each eye. No wonder these remarkable predators are called "mosquito hawks."

Dragonflies

26 With an adult, visit a pond or stream to look for dragonflies and damselflies. Do you know the difference? Dragonflies have larger bodies and hold their wings stretched out to the sides. Damselflies hold their wings together above their bodies.

27 Good luck trying to catch a dragonfly. They can fly forward and backward with amazing speed, and their huge eyes enable them to see movement in all directions. Be content to watch them. Look for a dragonfly flying backward, two dragonflies flying together (mating in flight), a dragonfly catching a mosquito or other prey in the air, and dragonflies of different colors.

28 If you hold a fishing pole or long branch over the water, a dragonfly may perch on it. Attach a fishing lure that looks like a dragonfly to your pole and dangle it near dragonflies. Do any of them defend their territory from the intruder-lure?

29 Use a net to scoop up a dragonfly or damselfly nymph in rotting leaves in shallow pond water. Nymphs look something like their parents, only uglier. A nymph is quite a predator, but it can be kept by itself in a small aquarium. (*See page 64 for directions.*) Be careful, nymphs can bite.

30 After several years, a nymph will climb out of the water and attach itself to a reed or stem. It sheds its skin for a final time and unfolds its wings to fly. Look for the empty skins and count them to get an idea of the dragonfly population. Maybe you will even see a dragonfly emerging on a still summer morning.

31 Collect a dragonfly stamp. There are more than 100 stamps from around the world featuring dragonflies.

19

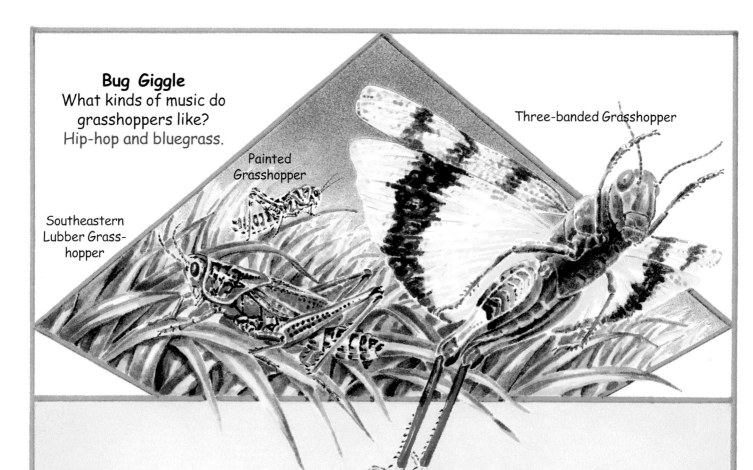

Bug Giggle
What kinds of music do grasshoppers like?
Hip-hop and bluegrass.

Painted Grasshopper

Three-banded Grasshopper

Southeastern Lubber Grass-hopper

Grasshoppers

Short-Horned Grasshoppers
(Class Insecta, Order Orthoptera)

Look for: An insect with long back legs and "knees" sticking up above its body, a long face, two pairs of wings, and a saddlelike cover behind its head. Different species range from ½"- 6".

Where to look: Fields of grass and weeds, lawns, quiet trails, and roadsides.

When to look: Spring, summer, and fall.

Range: Throughout the US.

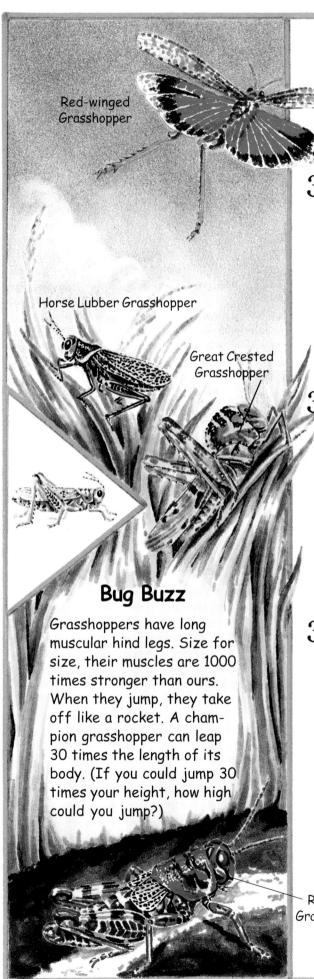

Red-winged Grasshopper

Horse Lubber Grasshopper

Great Crested Grasshopper

Bug Buzz

Grasshoppers have long muscular hind legs. Size for size, their muscles are 1000 times stronger than ours. When they jump, they take off like a rocket. A champion grasshopper can leap 30 times the length of its body. (If you could jump 30 times your height, how high could you jump?)

Rainbow Grasshopper

Grasshoppers

32 Catch a grasshopper and look it over. (Hold it between your finger and thumb, so that it can't bite you.) The two largest groups of grasshoppers are the short-horned grasshoppers and the long-horned grasshoppers. Short-horns have short antennae, usually less than half the length of their bodies. Long-horns have extremely long antennae, sometimes longer than their bodies. What kind of grasshopper did you catch? Look at page 12, "Anatomy of Insects." Can you name the parts of your grasshopper? Use a field guide to identify the grasshopper.

33 Plan a Grasshopper Field Day. Invite friends to catch a grasshopper and bring it to a paved driveway or play area. Use chalk to draw a large circle on the pavement. One at a time, have each person release his or her grasshopper from a starting point in the center of the circle. Use a stopwatch or a watch with a second hand to time how long it takes each grasshopper to get out of the circle. The winner is the grasshopper that gets away fastest.

34 Keep a grasshopper as a pet. Put about four inches of dirt in a terrarium that is at least 7" x 12". Collect leafy branches from the area where you caught the grasshopper and stick them into the dirt. Use a spray bottle to lightly mist the plants and dirt with water. Put your pet grasshopper in its new home. Cover the terrarium with a screen lid or with cheesecloth secured with a rubber band. Every day add fresh leaves and grass and more water from the spray bottle. You can also feed the grasshopper washed leafy vegetables from your kitchen, such as lettuce, cabbage, spinach, or celery.

21

Bug Giggle
How did the cricket
lose his voice?
He sprained his wing.

Snowy Tree
Cricket
(singing)

House
Cricket

Field Cricket

Crickets

Crickets (Class Insecta, Order Orthoptera)

Look for: An insect, often brown or black, with a broad body from ⅜"- 1" long
and with very long antennae. Two long cerci (feelers) extend at the end
of the abdomen. **Listen for:** High-pitched chirping.

Where to look: Bushy areas, weeds, and woods. House
crickets live indoors.

When to look and listen: Spring, summer, and fall.

Range: Throughout
the US.

Crickets

• • • • • • • • • • • • • •

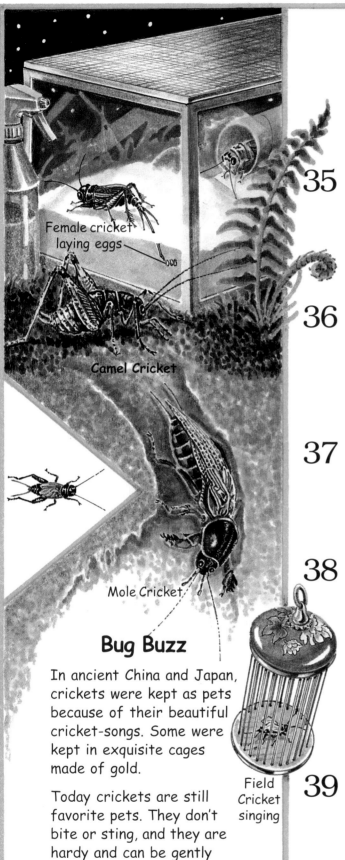

Female cricket laying eggs

Camel Cricket

Mole Cricket

Bug Buzz

In ancient China and Japan, crickets were kept as pets because of their beautiful cricket-songs. Some were kept in exquisite cages made of gold.

Today crickets are still favorite pets. They don't bite or sting, and they are hardy and can be gently handled without hurting them. Male crickets will either sing you to sleep— or keep you awake.

Field Cricket singing

35 Look for crickets in a pile of grass clippings or under a board left on the ground, or buy crickets at a pet store or bait shop. To make a cricket trap: (a) cut an unsliced loaf of bread in half; (b) scoop out the center; (c) tie the halves back together; (d) cut a one-inch hole in the bread to the center; (e) put the bread in the grass overnight; (f) look inside the loaf for crickets.

36 Examine a cricket through a magnifying lens. Is it male or female? Both have cerci, long feelers at the rear of their bodies, but females also have a spear-shaped ovipositor. Look for the cricket's ears, round organs just below its knees on each front leg!

37 Keep crickets in a terrarium or large jar with a lid. Add two inches of sand and small lengths of toilet paper rolls for "homes." Water with a mister and feed the crickets lettuce and dry cat food or bran.

38 To raise baby crickets, provide damp sand for the female to lay her eggs in. Dampen the sand every day and try to keep the temperature in the terrarium from 82-86 degrees with a 60-watt bulb nearby. When tiny crickets hatch from transparent eggs, move the adults to another container, so they don't eat the baby crickets.

39 A cricket "chirps" by rubbing its wings together. The warmer the temperature, the faster the chirp. You can tell the temperature of the air by counting the cricket chirps you hear in fifteen seconds and then adding forty to that number. The total should be the temperature in Fahrenheit degrees.

40 Put one male cricket in a container with a toilet-paper-roll "home." After two days, add another male. What happens? Chirping? Kicking? Head-butting? Wrestling?

Trickle Creek Books

Praying Mantis

Mantid
Egg Case

Carolina
Mantid

Praying Mantises

Praying Mantises
(Class Insecta, Order Mantodea)

Look for: A long slender insect (from 2-2½" long) with a triangular head, four thin legs, and two larger forelegs often held together as if in prayer. Green to brown and hard to see.

Where to look: Brushy meadows, on leaves and flowers.

When to look: Summer and fall.

Range: Eastern United States. (Other kinds of mantids can be found throughout the US.)

Note: *Is it legal to catch a praying mantis?*

Many people think that it is illegal to catch or kill a praying mantis. Praying mantises are beneficial to farmers, but they are not protected in the US — and never have been.

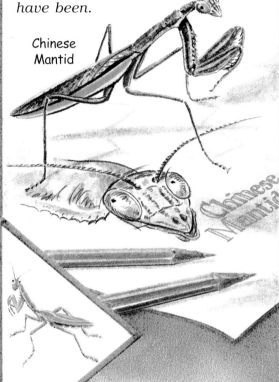

Chinese Mantid

Bug Buzz

Mantises are fierce predators and masters of disguise. Camouflaged as leaves, twigs, and flowers, they wait for their victims to come to them. Flower mantises look so much like flowers that they trick insects into landing on them to get nectar. Then the mantis grabs them. Large mantises even catch little frogs, lizards, and hummingbirds.

Orchid Mantid

Praying Mantises

· · · · · · · · · · · · ·

41 One fine day you'll come across a praying mantis. Do you see it praying? (Praying for prey?) Praying mantises hunt like cats by staying still and waiting for their prey, so you will have time to make a sketch or take some photographs.

42 Move slowly around the praying mantis and watch it watch you. The mantis can move its head 180 degrees.

43 Offer the mantis a drink of water from a spoon. Use tweezers to jiggle a piece of raw hamburger in front of the mantis. You may become fast friends.

44 Gently pick up the praying mantis. You may feel a pinch from its spiny forelegs. Put it on your arm. It may climb up on your shoulder.

45 Is your mantis a male or female? A female may be round and full of eggs. The male is a skinny stick. Count the segments on the underside of its abdomen. A female has five or six, a male has seven or eight. (Females are fierce: After mating, a female praying mantis may eat the male.)

46 Move a small twig suddenly toward a praying mantis. Does the mantis freeze in an upright position? Does it open its wings to look big and frightening? Does it strike?

47 Look for an *ootheca*, a mantis egg case, in the fall. (*Or see page 67 to order one.*) Refrigerate it until spring when prey is available. Feed the dozens of tiny mantises fruit flies or they will eat each other until only one is left.

Trickle Creek Books

Bug Giggle
What did one cicada say to another cicada who startled him?
"You scared me out of my skin!"

Periodical Cicada

Empty cicada shell

Dogday Harvestfly

Cicadas

Cicada
(Class Insecta, Order Homoptera)

Look for: A large, sturdy insect from 1- 2⅜" long with bulging eyes and long, clear wings. **Listen for:** An intense humming or buzzing that rises and falls during the day. Cicadas are quiet at night.

Where to look: Forests and grassy areas near trees.

When to look: Mid- to late summer.

Range: Throughout the US except for the Northwest.

Periodical Cicada

Bug Buzz

Some periodical cicadas live underground as nymphs for seventeen years. After they come out of the ground and become adults, they live another few weeks, just long enough to mate and for the females to lay eggs. These cicadas are not the longest living insects, but they live longer underground than any other insect.

Mud chimney

Cicadas

• • • • • • • • • • • •

48 In spring, cicada nymphs, which have lived underground for years, begin to tunnel to the surface. Look for half-inch holes in the ground. After heavy rains, the nymphs may build little mud chimneys, a kind of tunnel extension, to escape the high water. You can look for these, too.

49 When the soil warms up, cicadas begin to emerge from their tunnels. Use a flashlight to look for cicada nymphs at dusk or just after dark. The nymphs are wingless bugs with soft, milky white bodies. You may see them coming out of a hole or crawling along the ground.

50 If you keep a cicada nymph overnight, the following morning it will be an adult. Put smooth dirt in the bottom of a gallon jar or roomy terrarium, add several thick sticks in an upright position, and drop some wet leaves into the container. Pick up a nymph as gently as you can and place it in the container. Within hours, the cicada's wings will unfold and dry, its body will darken, and its shell will harden. During the night, the cicada will climb on one of the sticks and shed its skin. Set it free in the morning, so that it can mate.

51 It's fun to collect the skins shed by cicadas. Look on any vertical surface. You may also find dead cicadas on the ground. A jewelry box with a cotton lining and a clear plastic lid is a perfect place to keep them.

52 Cicadas don't bite or sting, but they have "sticky" feet with tiny claws. You can carry one around on your shoulder for a very long time.

53 Cicadas make a shrill buzzing noise. Watch a cicada vibrate when it buzzes.

27

Bug Giggle
Which bugs have the most horrendous manners? Spittlebugs. They're always spitting.

Saddled Leafhopper

Striped Green Leafhopper

Grape Leafhopper

Blue-green Sharpshooter

Red-banded Leafhopper

Rhododendron Leafhopper

Leafhoppers and Spittlebugs

Leafhoppers and Spittlebugs
(Class Insecta, Order Hemiptera)

Look for: Spittlebug. Small jumping insect ($1/8$"- $1/2$"), gray to brown, with short wings and antennae. **Leafhopper.** More slender and brightly colored with two rows of spines on hind legs. ($1/16$"- $5/8$" long.)

Where to look: Grassy meadows, fields of alfalfa and clover, shrubs and trees.

When to look: Spring and summer.

Range: Throughout the US.

Leafhoppers and Spittlebugs

Meadow Spittlebug nymph

Meadow Spittlebug

Black and Red Froghopper

Bug Buzz

There are more leafhopper species worldwide than all species of birds, mammals, reptiles, and amphibians combined. They are found from tropical rainforests to Arctic tundra.

In a field full of leafhoppers, there may be several million per acre. There is no excuse for not finding a leafhopper, but you can't keep them as pets. They need to jump from plant to plant, and each species needs a specific plant food and habitat.

54 Spittlebug nymphs cover themselves with bubbly, wet spittle to hide themselves from predators and to keep from drying out. Look for white "spit" on stems and grasses. Then gently blow the froth away to reveal one or two tiny pale nymphs, often feeding upside down. Once you find one mass of spittle, look for others nearby. *Note:* Nymphs may be light orange, yellow, or green.

55 Spittlebug nymphs often move from place to place as they feed. They just keep making their spitty covering wherever they go. If you have the patience, watch the nymphs you un-covered to see what they do next.

56 You can take a spittlebug nymph home, but you'll have to take its plant home too! Nymphs eat plant sap from living stems and leaves, so to keep these bugs, you must carefully dig up the plant it is on — roots and all — and replant it in a flowerpot with the bug still clinging to it. You won't need to "cage" the nymph and plant. The nymph will stay where it is as long as the plant is healthy. Be sure to water the plant and give it light.

57 Adult spittlebugs are often called "froghop-pers." Use an insect net to catch froghoppers and leafhoppers. Swing the net back and forth through the grasses and plants in a meadow. When you check the net, you'll know the little hoppers by their impressive hops. You'll get to know their shape too. They hold their wings over their bodies at an angle like the roof of a house. How many different kinds of hoppers did you catch?

58 Watch how the leafhoppers and froghoppers escape when you open the insect net. Do they run, hop, fly — or all three? Leafhoppers can run sideways. Did you see that?

Trickle Creek Books

Bug Giggle
What kind of bug will
shop till it drops?
A ladybug.

Three-banded
Ladybird Beetle

Polished Lady Beetle

Fifteen-spotted
Ladybird Beetle

Twice Stubbed
Ladybird Beetle

Seven-spotted Ladybird Beetle

Twelve-spotted
Ladybird Beetle

Ladybird Beetles and Aphids

Ladybird Beetle (Class Insecta, Order Coleoptera)
Aphid (Class Insecta, Order Homoptera)

Look for: Ladybug. A round, spotted beetle ($1/16$"- $3/8$"), red, orange, or yellow with black spots, or black with red or yellow spots. **Aphids.** Masses of tiny bugs with soft, pear-shaped bodies, often green, red, or brown.

Where to look for both ladybugs and aphids: On plants in fields and gardens. Swarms of ladybugs over-winter under fallen leaves or bark.

When to look: Spring through fall.

Range: Throughout the US.

Another Giggle
What do you call a sweet
little aphid?
An all-day sucker.

Ladybugs and Aphids

Aphids feeding

Ladybug Pupa

Convergent Ladybird Beetle

Ladybug Larva

Ladybug Eggs

Ash-gray Ladybird Beetle

Nine-spotted Ladybird Beetle

Bug Buzz

All summer, female aphids give birth to clones of themselves, all daughters. The daughters are born with their own daughters already growing inside them. In the fall, the females begin to have sons, too. Then males and females mate and females lay eggs, which overwinter. In spring when the eggs hatch, all the aphids that emerge will be females again. This is how aphids produce an amazing number of offspring. If it weren't for ladybugs and other aphid predators, we would be knee-deep in aphids. A ladybug can eat more than 100 aphids a day.

59 Aphids are little suckers that suck the life out of your garden. Look for them on the tender new growth of roses, lettuce, peas, or tomatoes. With a magnifying lens, you may see an aphid giving birth. (They're always giving birth!) Aphids reproduce so quickly and in such great numbers that they can destroy entire crops. They spread plant diseases too.

60 Can you prove that aphids are attracted to the color yellow? Put a yellow index card, and cards of other colors too, close to a plant with aphids on it. Are aphids drawn to the yellow card?

61 Wherever you find aphids, you may find a ladybug, because aphids are its favorite food. Look for ladybug eggs on the underside of leaves. They look like clusters of ten to fifteen tiny yellow cigars standing on end. Also look for ladybug larvae, which are like spiny black alligators with bright markings. They eat aphids too.

62 If you find a "dead" ladybug, watch it for a while. Ladybugs defend themselves by falling to the ground and appearing dead. Was it just playing dead?

63 You can keep a ladybug in a jar for a week if you care for it carefully. Give it half a raisin for food each day. Soften and plump the raisin by soaking it in water for ten minutes. Give your ladybug water with a damp paper towel, not drops of water. Put fresh leaves in the jar for shelter.

64 When you find a ladybug, count its spots and note its color. There are hundreds of different species of ladybugs. Some even have stripes or no spots at all.

Trickle Creek Books

Bug Giggle
What does a firefly like to eat?
Light snacks.

Pyralis Firefly

Pyralis Firefly

Fireflies

Firefly (Class Insecta, Order Coleoptera)

Look for: A long, dark, soft-bodied beetle ($\frac{3}{8}$"- $\frac{5}{8}$") with a "taillight" at the tip of its abdomen that flashes green or yellow. Its wing covers are black, edged in yellow along the sides.

Where to look: Meadows or lawns, open woods, backyards and gardens.

When to look: Summer evenings after dark.

Range: In the US, east of the Rocky Mountains.

Another Giggle
How do fireflies start a race?
Ready, set, glow!

Pyralis
Firefly

Bug Buzz

A female predator firefly called *Photuris* can mimic the flash of other firefly species. When a male blinks, she blinks right back in the same pattern, but when he comes to her, she eats him.

Fireflies

65 Fireflies flash each other coded messages to find mates. The male signals as he flies. Then the female answers from her perch on a tall grass stem or bush. See if you can attract a firefly with a small flashlight (a penlight is best). Watch a firefly carefully. Two seconds after it flashes, give a quick flash with your penlight. Keep responding to the firefly to catch its interest.

66 Catch fireflies and keep them in a jar. Put the jar of fireflies outside to see if they attract others or if they warn others with a distress signal. Or keep them in your room after you go to bed and watch the fireflies in the dark. Release them in the morning.

67 A lightbulb gives off much more heat than light, but the energy in firefly light is called "cold light" because it gives off very little heat. Fireflies light up by mixing chemicals in their bodies. One of the chemicals, *luciferin*, can be made in a laboratory and is used in light sticks. Buy a light stick at a sporting goods store or a toy store to see how chemicals can mix together to give off light without giving off heat.

68 Everyone knows that fireflies glow, but did you know that their eggs and larvae can glow, too? The firefly larvae, which look something like mealworms, are called glowworms. Look for glowworms at night in moist places under leaf litter or decaying bark.

69 Look for a frog with a glowing throat or lit-up eardrums. That's what happens to a frog that eats too many fireflies!

Trickle Creek Books

Bug Giggle
Why did the beetle always
hang out with the same
group of friends?
He was a clique beetle.

Black and White
Click Beetle

Black-tailed
Click Beetle

Lantern
Click Beetle

Eyed Click Beetle

Click Beetles

Click Beetles
(Class Insecta, Order Coleoptera)

Look for: Tiny to medium-sized beetles ($1/16$"- 2") with long, flat, straight-sided bodies. Eyed click beetles have ringed eyespots on the thorax.

Where to look: Trees and plants in woods or near decaying wood and wood piles.

When to look: Spring to fall.

Range: Throughout the US.

Click Beetles

70 Look for click beetles in a wood pile, under decaying bark, on the trunks of fruit trees, on leaves of trees and bushes, or near outside lights at night. If you find an eyed click beetle, look closely at its eyespots. Do you think those glaring "eyes" could startle an enemy? Do they make the beetle look big?

71 Pick up a click beetle and hold it in your hand. It won't hurt you. If the click beetle rolls over and plays dead, see if its legs and antennae fold up against its body. Would playing dead protect the click beetle from predators that only eat live insects?

72 While the click beetle plays dead, look carefully at the underside of the beetle's thorax for a spine, which points toward the rear of the bug and fits into a groove on the abdomen. This is the snapping mechanism that enables the click beetle to click and leap into the air.

73 Hold the click beetle in your open palm until you hear a CLICK and see the beetle flip into the air. How high did it go? Did it surprise you? Did it get away from you? If the click beetle landed on its back, wait for it to click and flip again.

74 Keep a click beetle (or several) in a small terrarium with a screen lid. Add a damp paper towel or use a spray mister for water. Give the click beetles fresh leaves and flowers to eat, although some click beetles don't eat at all.

75 If you live in the deep South in the United States, you might find a Lantern Click Beetle. Put the beetle in a jar with a damp, crumpled paper towel. After dark, the beetle will light up the jar like a lantern with light organs on its thorax and abdomen.

Groove   Spine

Click Beetle playing dead

Bug Buzz

In a moment, a click beetle can go from playing dead to hurling itself up to twelve inches into the air. It gains speed from a standstill faster than any other leaping animal in the world — faster than a frog, faster than a leopard, faster than a monkey or a lemur.

35

Bug Giggle
How is a whirligig beetle
like a child at a fair?
It loves a merry
go-round.

Large Whirligig

Small Whirligig

Whirligig Beetles
(Class Insecta, Order Coleoptera)

Look for: A tiny, shiny black beetle ($\frac{1}{8}$"- $\frac{5}{8}$") that looks like a watermelon seed. It swims in circles on the surface of water. Often in groups.

Where to look: Near the edges of ponds, lakes, and slow streams.

When to look: Late summer and fall.

Range: Throughout the US.

Note: *Take an adult with you when you explore near water.*

Upper portion of left eye

Lower portion of left eye

Bug Buzz

Whirligig beetles have enemies both in and out of the water, but these wily little creatures can keep an eye out for a heron and a fish at the same time.

Whirligigs have compound eyes that are divided into two, with one pair above the water and one pair below. So they can see both above and below the water surface.

Whirligig Beetles

76 Look for whirligigs at the edge of a pond or stream. Do you see them spinning around on the surface? Do they always turn in the same direction or do they change direction?

77 Do you see more than one whirligig? If you find a group, try to guess or measure the width of the cluster of beetles. Some groups are several feet across. Do you see any beetles bumping into each other?

78 What happens when you disturb the whirligigs? Do they dive? Or fly? Or bunch together and swim in circles? Or all three?

79 Use a long-handled dip net to catch some whirligigs — if you can. See why they whirl?

80 Put the whirligigs in a jar half-full of pond water and quickly put a lid on the jar. (They can fly.) If you see a beetle dive down to the bottom of the jar, look for an air bubble at the tip of its abdomen. This air supply enables whirligigs to stay underwater for a long time.

81 Catch a whirligig with your hands. Then smell your hands. A Large Whirligig (a species that is more than ⅜" long) has a fruity smell like an apple. A Small Whirligig (a species less than ¼" long) smells terrible.

82 Keep whirligigs in an aquarium with a lid. Provide a stick that extends out of the water for them to climb on. Feed them live or dead insects. Drop a dead moth into the water. What happens? Put a tiny bit of raw fish in the water. Fish are enemies of whirligigs. Do the beetles dive or fly to avoid the fish?

83 Make a whirligig raft from a chip of unpainted weathered wood, so your beetles can climb out of the water.

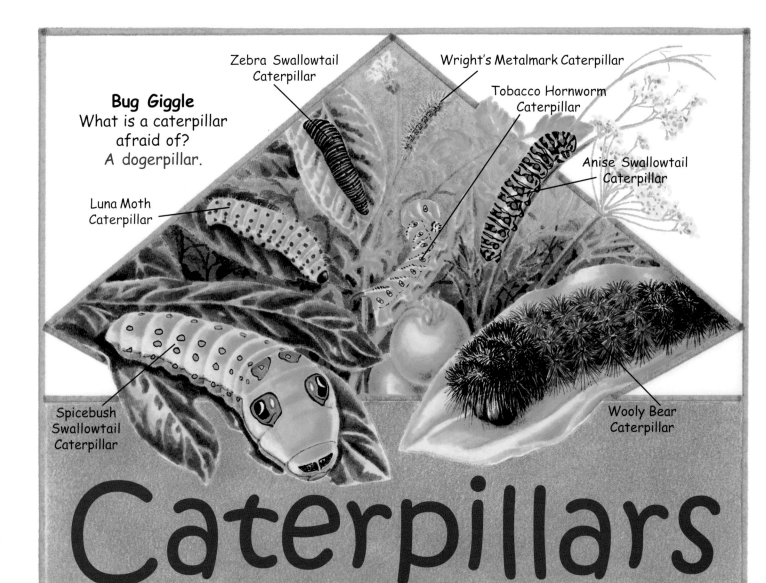

Bug Giggle
What is a caterpillar
afraid of?
A dogerpillar.

Zebra Swallowtail
Caterpillar

Wright's Metalmark Caterpillar

Tobacco Hornworm
Caterpillar

Anise Swallowtail
Caterpillar

Luna Moth
Caterpillar

Spicebush
Swallowtail
Caterpillar

Wooly Bear
Caterpillar

Caterpillars

Caterpillars
(Class Insecta, Order Lepidoptera)

Look for: Larvae of butterflies and moths with soft wormlike bodies, powerful jaws, six true legs on the thorax, and up to ten false legs on the abdomen.

Where to look: Orchards, gardens, and forest edges.

When to look: Spring through fall, especially late spring.

Range: Throughout US.

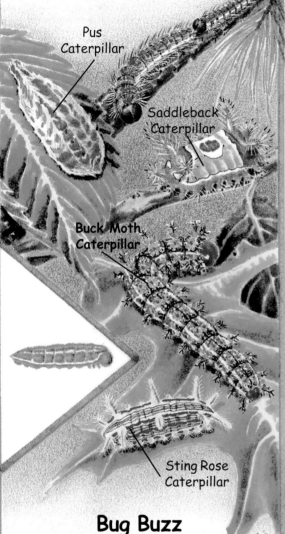

Pus Caterpillar

Saddleback Caterpillar

Buck Moth Caterpillar

Sting Rose Caterpillar

Pine Processionary Caterpillars

Io Moth caterpillar

Bug Buzz

Caterpillars are eating machines. Their over-lapping jaws cut leaves like sharp scissors. Grinding plates mash the leaves into a pulp. They shed their skins over and over as they grow at an amazing rate.

A Tobacco Hornworm will increase its weight 10,000 times in less than twenty days. A Monarch caterpillar will increase its body mass 30,000 times.

Caterpillars

• • • • • • • • • • • •

84 Caterpillars are messy eaters. When you see chewed leaves and caterpillar poop, called *frass*, you'll be on the trail of a caterpillar. The frass looks like peppercorns. Spend some time watching a caterpillar crawl or eat.

85 Many caterpillars feed at night. Look for them with a flashlight on a nighttime walk.

86 Place a caterpillar on the rim of a flower pot. Does it crawl around the rim? How many times? When you get tired of watching, put the caterpillar back where you found it.

87 You may find a Wooly Bear Caterpillar crossing a road in late fall. It is black with a band of red-brown bristles around its middle. You can hold it in your palm. According to folk lore, the more black on the caterpillar, the colder the coming winter will be.

88 Hold a two-foot length of cotton string so that it hangs down but doesn't touch the ground. Place a caterpillar at the bottom of the string. Time its climb to the top. Hold a race with two pieces of string and two caterpillars.

89 A caterpillar garden is different from a butterfly garden. Butterflies like flowers with nectar, but some good plants for caterpillars are cabbage, carrot, dill, parsley, hollyhocks, willows, and wisteria. Find out which butterflies are common in your yard. Then plant the specific plants that their caterpillars need.

90 Tent caterpillars spin a silken tent to protect them from birds. Break off a tree branch with tent caterpillars on it and prop it in a bucket overnight. What do you see in the morning?

91 Keep a caterpillar journal with sketches or photos of caterpillars you see. Include notes about where and when they were found.

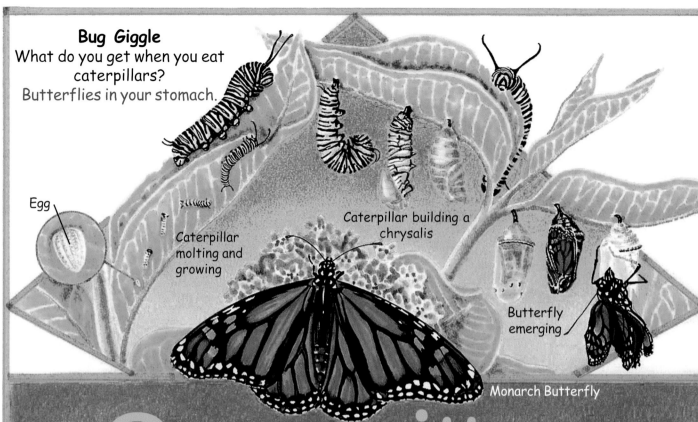

Bug Giggle
What do you get when you eat caterpillars?
Butterflies in your stomach.

Egg

Caterpillar molting and growing

Caterpillar building a chrysalis

Butterfly emerging

Monarch Butterfly

Caterpillars to Butterflies

Caterpillars to Butterflies and Moths

Life cycle: Complete metamorphosis with four stages: egg, larva (caterpillar), pupa (cocoon or chrysalis), and adult.

Look for: Caterpillars or pupae. A moth pupa is often wrapped in a silk cocoon, which the caterpillar spins around itself. A butterfly pupa has a hardened skin, a protective shell called a chrysalis.

Where to look for pupae: Attached to a leaf, twig, bark, or rough surface; in crevices or soil.

When to look: All seasons.

Range: Throughout the US.

Note: *If you order caterpillars from a biological supply company, make sure the butterflies are native to your area and that they will be released when the weather is warm and flowers are blooming.*

Cecropia Moth

Cecropia Moth Cocoon

Isabella Moth Cocoon (Wooly Bear)

Bug Buzz

Caterpillars are picky eaters:

Monarch Butterfly Caterpillars only eat milkweeds.

Tomato Hornworms like tomato plants.

Cabbageworms eat plants in the cabbage family.

Luna Moth Caterpillars eat leaves from walnut, hickory, sweet gum, and persimmon trees.

Wooly Bear Caterpillars eat plantain leaves or dandelion leaves.

Eastern Black Swallowtail Caterpillars eat parsley, dill, and fennel.

Caterpillars to Butterflies

92 You can buy caterpillars from a biological supply company, which come with a container and a supply of food. Your part is to watch the caterpillars grow, build their cocoons or chrysalises, and emerge as new creatures!

93 Give yourself two assignments: Keep a record of the changes that occur. And find out where the butterflies live naturally, so that you can release them in the right habitat.

94 It's fun to raise a "wild" caterpillar that you find yourself, but first you must observe it carefully and find out *exactly* what it eats. It will not grow without the correct plants to feed on. Check an insect field guide, too.

95 Keep your caterpillar in a terrarium with a screen lid or in a large jar covered with netting. Put soil in the bottom of the container with some tiny branches and a piece of bark. Keep the container outside in natural temperature and light. Don't move the container after the caterpillar becomes a pupa.

96 Twice a day, provide a fresh supply of the right plants for your caterpillar. Pick leaves on stems and sprinkle a little water on them. Every few days, empty the container and rinse it well. Replace the caterpillar and add fresh leaves and soil.

97 If you find a cocoon or chrysalis, don't remove it from the twig it is attached to. Put the twig and the cocoon into your terrarium in the same position in which you found them.

98 When the butterfly or moth emerges, it will need room to spread its wings and dry them. Provide twigs for the butterfly to climb on or its wings may be deformed. Release it as soon as it is ready to fly, so that it doesn't injure its wings. Release it under a bush for shelter.

Buckeye Butterfly

Tiger Swallowtail Butterfly

Bug Giggle
Why couldn't the butterfly go to the dance? Because it was a moth ball.

Red-spotted Purple Butterfly

Hackberry Butterfly

Butterflies and Moths

Butterflies and Moths
(Class Insecta, Order Lepidoptera)

Look for: Insects with large eyes and four wings covered with tiny colored scales (wingspan from ½"- 11⅛"). Most adults have a long tongue like a coiled tube.

Where to look: Woods, meadows, gardens, wetlands.

When to look: Spring through fall, all year in south Texas and Florida.

Range: Throughout US.

Another Giggle
What do moths study in school? Mothematics.

Luna Moth

Wooly Bear
Caterpillar Moth

Bug Buzz

The North American Pygmy Blue, with a wingspan of ¹/₂", is the smallest butterfly in the world.

Pygmy Blue
Butterfly

The largest is the Queen Alexandra's Birdwing in New Guinea. It has a wing-span up to 11³/₈", almost a foot across! It was first collected when someone shot it down from the rainforest canopy. Maybe they thought it was a large bird.

Butterflies/Moths

99 Plant a butterfly garden to attract butterflies to your yard. Choose a sunny location and plant flowers rich in nectar, such as butterfly bushes, lilacs, zinnias, phlox, bee balm, lantanas, and marigolds. Include flat rocks where butterflies can sun themselves.

100 Make a shallow, damp mud puddle for male butterflies. They will land on the mud to take in salts that they need.

101 Butterflies are active during the day, while most moths are active at night. Attract moths to a "shining sheet" by hanging a white sheet over a railing or between two trees. Set up a flashlight behind it. Then sit quietly in front of the sheet and watch for visitors. Are moths as brightly colored as butterflies? Notice their plump bodies and feathery antennae.

102 Sometimes a butterfly will land on you. When you see a butterfly feeding, approach it slowly and gently hold out one finger near its legs. In the eastern and southern United States, the Hackberry Butterfly often lands on people. It's fun to hold a butterfly on your finger, but don't touch its fragile wings.

103 Some Monarch butterflies migrate almost 2000 miles. Follow the monarchs online at Journey North, www.learner.org/jnorth/.

104 Visit a butterfly exhibit at a botanical garden, zoo, or nature center. Watch butterflies eat and fly. Which is your favorite? Does the exhibit also have caterpillars and chrysalises?

105 Make a "Butterfly Field Guide to My Backyard." Allow at least one page for each butterfly. Include the name of the butterfly, a sketch or photo, information that you gather, and notes about your own observations.

Ants
(Class Insecta, Order Hymenoptera)

Look for: Black, brown, or reddish insects ($\frac{1}{16}$"- 1") with large heads, slender waists, and antennae bent like elbows. Very active.

Where to look: Near ant mounds in loose soil, in dead wood, and under rocks or boards.

When to look: Spring through fall.

Range: Throughout the US.

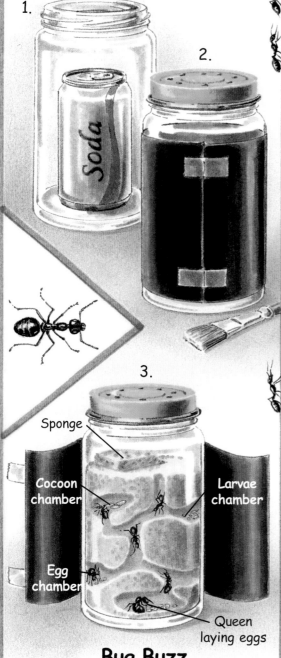

1.

2.

Soda

3.

Sponge

Cocoon chamber

Larvae chamber

Egg chamber

Queen laying eggs

Bug Buzz

Tropical Army Ants march in an army of millions, up to sixty-five feet across, and eat almost anything in their path, including small animals.

Ants

106 Find ants in an ant hill or under a log or rock. Or attract them with cookie-bait. Use a magnifying lens to observe them. Often ants are different shapes and sizes. Small workers gather food, clean the nest, care for the queen, or babysit. Soldiers with big heads defend the nest. The giant queen lays eggs.

107 Pick up an ant from an ant trail by letting it crawl on a leaf you are holding. Then put the ant down near the trail. Does it return to the trail? (Ants follow a chemical scent trail put down by the ants in front of them.) Try to interrupt the ant trail. Put a rock on the trail. Or dig a tiny ditch across the trail and pour water into it. What do the ants do?

108 Set up an ant habitat to watch the remarkable way that ants live and work together. Use a paintbrush to push about 30 ants into a jar. Quickly put the lid on the jar. Or with the help of an adult, dig up a colony with a trowel. If you collect tiny white eggs, ant larvae (white grubs), ant pupae (sometimes in cocoons), or the queen, you will have an especially interesting habitat.

109 Put your ants in the refrigerator to slow them down while you prepare their habitat: Put an unopened soft drink can inside a large glass jar to force the ants to tunnel where you can see them. Add soil and ants around the can. Put a moist sponge on top of the soil and keep it moist every day. Put holes in the lid.

110 Feed the ants every few days, paying attention to what they like. Try bits of fruit, cheese, vegetables, meat, dead insects, bread, and honey. Remove uneaten food each day.

111 Wrap the jar with black paper to encourage the ants to tunnel against the sides of the jar. Remove the paper to observe the ants.

Trickle Creek Books

Fruit Flies

Fruit Flies

Fruit Flies
(Class Insecta, Order Diptera)

Look for: Tiny yellow or brown flies ($\frac{1}{16}$"- $\frac{1}{8}$"), often with red eyes. Their wings cross over their abdomens.

Where to look: Near decaying fruit; the larvae are found in the flesh of the rotting fruit.

When to look: Summer and fall.

Range: Throughout the US.

Common fruit flies are called drosophila. Look in your field guide for *Drosophila melanogaster.*

Eggs

Pupae

Larvae

Day 1: trapped 11 fruit flies.

Bug Buzz

Scientists throughout the world study fruit flies. Their extremely short life cycle of 10-14 days makes fruit flies perfect for studying genetics (how traits such as eye color are passed from parents to offspring). Researchers even conduct experiments with fruit flies on the Space Shuttle and International Space Station to study the possible effects of space travel on humans.

Fruit Flies

112 Order fruit flies from a biological supply company (*see page 67*), or trap your own. Mash very ripe bananas. Add water and a bit of baker's yeast. Place the mixture in the bottom of a quart jar. Place the open jar-trap on its side in a warm, shady spot outside, or better, near a garbage can or compost pile.

113 After one to three days, when fruit flies are attracted to the banana mixture, sneak up on them slowly. Then quickly trap them by pulling a piece of fabric over the mouth of the jar. Secure it with a wide rubber band. Make a note of the date.

114 Observe the fruit flies carefully. Make a list of ten things you see, including how the flies look, how they act, and where they gather in the jar. Use a magnifying lens to see them. Make sketches to back up your observations.

115 Observe the fruit flies every day for two weeks. Each day, record the date and add something new to your list.

116 If you have a dozen fruit flies in your jar, some will surely be females, which will lay eggs on the banana mixture. The eggs will be too tiny to see easily, but if you put a small piece of black paper down, you may see them.

117 The eggs will hatch in one day into tiny white worms (larvae). By the fifth day, you should be able to see them wiggling in the banana goo. Look through the sides of the jar.

118 A day or two later, the worms will climb onto the sides of the jar and become pupae. Their skins will harden into a tough red-brown casing, and inside the casing, the worms will change into flies. A few days later, the casing will split open and new fruit flies will emerge. How long did the entire life cycle take?

Bug Giggle
What bug has trouble finding pants that fit?
Daddy longlegs.

Eastern
Daddy Longlegs

Daddy
Longlegs

Daddy Longlegs
(Class Arachnida, Order Opiliones)

Look for: An insect-like animal with eight long thin legs and a tiny round body, $\frac{1}{4}$" to $\frac{3}{8}$". Eastern Daddy Longlegs have greenish-brown bodies; Brown Daddy Longlegs have reddish-brown bodies.

Where to look: Open ground and tree trunks. Shady walls of buildings and under decks or logs.

When to look: Most common in fall.

Range: Brown Daddy Longlegs through-out the US.

Daddy Longlegs

Brown Daddy Longlegs

Royal Moth

Eastern Daddy Longlegs

119 Find a daddy longlegs. It has eight hair-thin legs like a spider but no waist and no web. It walks with its body close to the ground and its "knees" up high. (Sometimes a cellar spider or a crane fly is called a daddy longlegs, but cellar spiders have narrow waists and crane flies have wings and six legs.)

120 To catch a daddy longlegs, let it climb onto your palm. Then gently close your hand around it. Be careful of its legs, which easily break off. Daddy long legs won't hurt you but they do stink a little. They have scent glands that give off an odd smell to warn predators that they might taste odd too. Do you smell anything on your hand?

121 Make a flowerpot trap. Put a clay flowerpot on its side in a shady flower bed. Daddy longlegs are nocturnal (active at night). During the day, they like to rest in a cool protected place. Check the flowerpot everyday to see if a daddy longlegs is hiding in it. If not, you should at least find a slug or snail or some other tiny animal.

122 Look for a tangle of daddy longlegs hiding in a cool, dark place. If you find them clustered together this way, see if you can count them.

123 Daddy longlegs are also called "harvestmen," "daddy longleggers," "father longlegs," "Harry longlegs," "shepherd spiders," and "grand-daddy longlegs." Can you make up another name?

124 Keep a daddy longlegs in a terrarium. Feed it little bits of juicy fruits and vegetables, oatmeal, or dead insects. After your pet eats, watch it clean its long legs, especially the second pair of legs used as feelers.

Bug Buzz

If a predator grabs a daddy longlegs and pulls off one of its legs, the leg will twitch and move for a minute...or several minutes...or even up to an hour. Can you imagine the predator staring at the twitching leg while the daddy longlegs makes its escape?

Note: *Don't pull a leg from any tiny animal. You know better.*

Bug Giggle
What do you get when you cross
a millipede with a parrot?
A walkie-talkie.

Californiulus euphanus

Kentucky Flat Millipede

Florida Black/White Millipede

Narceus americanus

Millipedes

Millipedes (Class Diplopoda)

Look for: A small crawling animal with a long segmented body and two pairs of legs on most of the segments. Its body is covered with a hard shell. Millipedes vary in color but many are black or brown.

Where to look: Under damp logs and rocks, under the bark of logs and stumps.

When to look: Spring through fall.

Range: Throughout the US.

Millipedes

* Have short legs and move slowly
* Have two pairs of legs per body segment
* Have more legs than centipedes do
* Glide and flow along
* Are tube-shaped
* Have short antennae
* Are gentle vegetarians

Centipedes

* Have long legs and are very quick
* Have one pair of legs per body segment
* Wiggle along with an S-shaped motion
* Are flat and wide
* Have long antennae
* Bite! *(Some are poisonous.)*

Pill Millipede

Bug Buzz

The Pill Millipede is found in the southern US. When it is attacked, it oozes a special chemical that makes its attacker sleepy. The pill millipede can put a Wolf Spider to sleep for 12 hours. Maybe it should be called a Sleeping-pill Millipede!

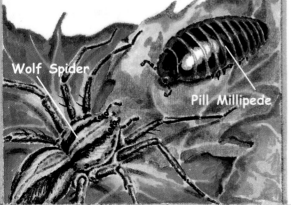

Wolf Spider

Pill Millipede

Millipedes

125 Look for millipedes under damp rocks and rotting logs. Watch for centipedes. They bite! Gently guide a millipede into a bug jar and then replace any rocks or logs that you have disturbed.

126 Buy a millipede. It may sound strange to save your allowance to buy a bug, but wouldn't you love to have a bright red and black Fire Millipede from Madagascar or a Giant Banded Millipede from Africa? (*See page 67.*)

127 Put your millipedes in a container with a tight lid, because they can escape. Put two inches of soil in the bottom, then a layer of leaf litter, especially oak leaves. (Many millipedes need oak leaves in order to grow.) Mist their habitat everyday. Feed them decaying plant matter, such as an apple core or rotting leaves.

128 Make a millipede cave, so your millipedes have a cozy place to hide. Glue several small rocks together to form the cave or provide a rounded piece of bark.

129 Watch for baby millipedes as small as commas. After molting, the babies are whitish and easy to spot.

130 Design an experiment to find out what millipedes prefer: light or dark, damp or dry, an open space or a hiding place.

131 Gently poke a millipede with a soft paintbrush. Does the millipede run away? Play dead? Curl up? Stink? (Most millipedes can give off a bad smell.)

132 Spread a very thin layer of jelly or honey on a piece of paper. Let your millipede walk on it. Then watch to see if it will clean all those feet with its mouth.

Trickle Creek Books

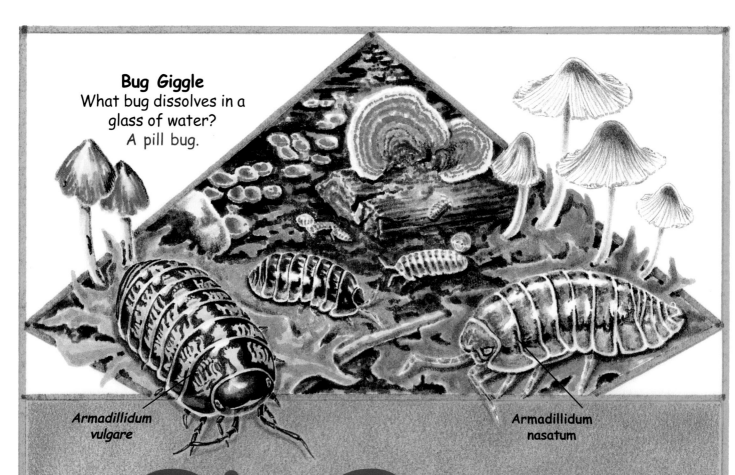

Bug Giggle
What bug dissolves in a
glass of water?
A pill bug.

*Armadillidum
vulgare*

*Armadillidum
nasatum*

Pill Bugs

Pill Bugs
(Class Crustacea, Order Isopoda)

Look for: A gray, oval, insect-like animal ($\frac{1}{4}$" to $\frac{1}{2}$") with fourteen legs, sharply angled antennae, and seven "armored plates" on its back. Pill bugs roll into a ball when disturbed.

Where to look: In damp places — under rotting logs or rocks, under grass clippings or leaf litter.

When to look: Spring through fall.

Range: Throughout most of the US.

Pill Bugs

Sowbug

Taillike appendages

Pill Bug

Head

Rear end

Bug Buzz

A pill bug is a little armored creature with overlapping plates on its body, which enable it to roll into a tight ball when it is threatened — just like an armadillo. You can see why one family of pill bugs is called Armadilli-didae. A pill bug's armor is tough enough to withstand the jaws of a praying mantis.

Three-banded Armadillo

133 To catch pill bugs, make a potato trap. Scoop out a tunnel part way into a raw potato. Place the potato trap under damp leaf litter. Keep it damp for several days. Look inside the potato for pill bugs that have come to dine.

134 Are pill bugs insects? Count their legs. To find out if you have a pill bug or a sowbug, give your bug a "tail test." Sowbugs have two tail-like appendages on their rear ends. Pill bugs don't. Pill bugs can roll up into a tight ball. Sowbugs can't.

135 Use a small paintbrush to tickle your pill bugs. Some pill bugs (rollers) will roll up into a ball. Some (hikers) will quickly walk away. How many of each do you have?

136 Set up a pill bug habitat in a terrarium. (*See page 65.*) You can add millipedes, crickets, and snails to make a very lively community. Watch your pill bugs during the day, but check them at night too when are they most active.

137 If you take good care of your pill bugs, you can expect pill bug babies. The young hatch in their mother's brood pouch and stay there for several weeks. Look for tiny white babies.

138 Pill bugs are crustaceans like shrimp and crabs, only they live on land. They still breathe through gill-like structures and will die if they dry out. Experiment to see if they prefer a damp environment. Tape two pieces of paper toweling about one-half inch apart in the bottom of a plastic container. Wet one paper and keep one dry. Put some pill bugs between the papers and see which they prefer.

139 Place a pill bug on damp soil in a container. Then put the container in sunlight. Your pill bug will want to get away from the light and heat, which are drying. What does it do?

Trickle Creek Books

Bug Giggle
Where does a spider
hang out?
At its favorite web site.

Orb Web

Garden Spider

American
House
Spider

Cobweb

Egg
Sack

Sheet
Web

Funnel
Web

Grass Spider

Hammock Spider

Spiders and Webs

Spiders (Class Arachnida, Order Araneae)

Look for: An insect-like animal with eight legs, eight eyes, two body parts with a "waist," and fangs.

Where to look for spiders: On the ground, under rocks, on plants. **Where to look for webs:** On the ground, between branches, in grass, in dark corners inside.

When to look: All year, especially fall.

Range: Throughout the US.

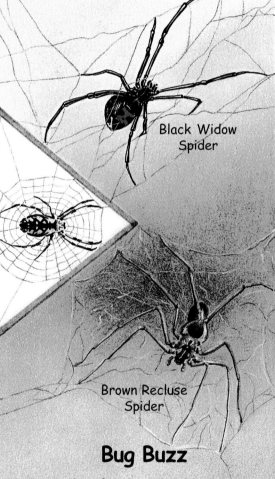

Black Widow Spider

Brown Recluse Spider

Bug Buzz

Spiders have spinnerets on their rear ends, which spin out silk. A single spider can spin different kinds of silk for different purposes: for traps and nets, ropes for binding prey, safety lines and parachutes, egg sacs, and nests and sleeping bags. Spider silk is stronger than steel of the same thickness.

Spider Webs

140 Look for spider webs in corners both inside and outside. Look under a porch, in the lawn, in a garden. Draw a picture or take a photo of a spider web. Is it an orb web, a funnel web, a sheet web, or a cobweb?

141 Once you locate a spider web, keep an eye on it for several days. Some spiders retract their old webs and make new ones at night. It's wonderful to watch a spider build its web.

142 Check a spider web after it rains to see it lined with water droplets.

143 Spiders are predators that eat insects. Look for insects caught in the spider web. An orb web is perfect for trapping flying insects; a funnel web or a sheet web catches crawling insects; a cobweb may net both flying and crawling insects. Are any of the insects tied up with spider silk like a package?

144 Look for the spider that made the web, but don't touch the spider. Jiggle the web with a tiny twig to draw the spider from its hiding place. Does the spider rush to the part of the web touched by the twig?

145 Collect a length of spider silk from a web. Gently stretch it. How far will it stretch before breaking? Spider silk is stretchier than rubber. It only breaks when it is stretched two to four times its length.

146 To collect a web, locate one that can be reached from both front and back. Scare the spider away. (It will make a new web.) Then lightly spray one side of the web with black spray paint. Spray the other side of the web with spray glue. Bring a piece of white paper against the sticky side of the web, so that the web sticks to the paper. To save the web, cover the paper with clear contact paper.

The Bug Band

· · · · · · · · · · · · · · · ·

Insects have many voices. Some insects make a sound when you pick them up. A Hissing Cockroach hisses, of course. A click beetle clicks. A long-horned beetle cries. A bessbug squeaks. And a Death's Head Hawk Moth can make a sound like a human voice. All of these sounds may alarm or even threaten a predator and allow the insect to escape.

Sometimes insects sing to attract a mate or frighten a rival. They may sing to stake a claim to a certain small place as their home. Crickets chirp, cicadas buzz, and katydids call, "Katy did, Katy didn't." The sounds they make are not necessarily made with their voices. For example, crickets "sing" by rubbing their wings together. Hissing Cockroaches push air out of breathing holes in their sides. And cicadas produce their chain-saw sounds with drumlike membranes on either side of their abdomens. A male cicada can belt out a song louder than a vacuum cleaner.

When all the bugs sing together, the bug band has a steady rhythm, lots of insect players, and very high volume. Wouldn't summer be dull without bug song?

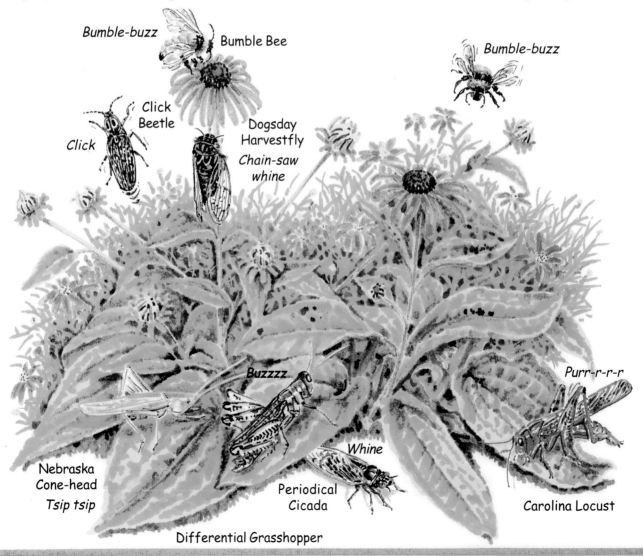

Bumble-buzz — Bumble Bee

Bumble-buzz

Click — Click Beetle

Dogsday Harvestfly — Chain-saw whine

Buzzzz

Purr-r-r-r

Whine

Nebraska Cone-head

Tsip tsip

Periodical Cicada

Carolina Locust

Differential Grasshopper

Bug Song

· · · · · · · · · · · · · ·

Gladiator Katydid

True Katydid

Chirp, Chirp
I hear the bugs
Singing their song.
I can't wait
anymore,
So I start to
sing along.

Chirp-chirp-chirp

Field Cricket

147 Go outside on a late summer night to listen to the bug band. Do you hear insect voices? Can you tell them apart? Can you tell where they are coming from? Take a flashlight and see how close you can get to a singing bug before it stops singing.

148 Write a poem or song or story about the bug band. Then record yourself reading what you wrote, but make your recording outside when insects are singing. Let the real bug band be the background for your creative writing. How does it sound?

149 Make a recording of grasshoppers singing. They are calling their mates. Then play your recording at high volume back to the grasshoppers. Did the recording attract any female grasshoppers?

150 Catch or buy a few crickets. Prepare a small terrarium with a layer of sand in the bottom, water from a spray bottle, some bits of bread, and two "cricket houses." The cricket houses can be made by cutting an empty toilet paper roll into two-inch lengths. Put two male crickets in the terrarium. (You can tell male and female crickets apart because a female has an ovipositor, or egg depositor, projecting from the back of her abdomen. It looks like a slender sword.) Give the two male crickets several days to settle into their homes in the terrarium. Then add a third male cricket to the terrarium. Often the first two crickets will chirp loudly and aggressively to challenge the intruder. They are telling him, "This is *our* home. You don't belong here."

Poem by Avery Van Etten, age 9

Trickle Creek Books

Bug Olympics

If the world held a Bug Olympics, we would be amazed by astounding athletic feats and new and different world records set by tiny competitors. Of course there would be gold medals for strength and speed and agility, but there would be new categories of competition, too, like the most explosive bug and the best glue stick....

Wouldn't it be fun to watch the Bug Olympics?

Best Glue Stick ● Weaver Ant Larva

Weaver Ants build their nests by rolling up leaves and sticking them together. They get the "glue" they need by picking up a larva and squeezing its abdomen to make it produce a sticky silk thread. The larva isn't hurt and doesn't struggle. Maybe it likes being a glue stick.

Coolest Bug ● Wooly Bear Caterpillar

A Wooly Bear Caterpillar can survive an Arctic winter with temperatures as low as -90 degrees. The caterpillar produces a natural antifreeze that enables it to slowly become frozen except for the very innermost part of its cells. In the spring, it thaws out and crawls away.

Fastest Sprinter ● Tiger Beetle

A Tiger Beetle, the fastest insect on earth, can run two feet per second, which is only 1.5 miles per hour, but if the beetle were as big as a horse, its speed would be 250 miles per hour.

Worst Dressed Bug ● Assassin Bug Nymph

The Assassin Bug nymph dresses itself in sand grains and dead ants. Its outfit isn't very attractive, but it provides good camouflage and attracts other ants, which the Assassin Bug is glad to eat.

Most Explosive Bug ● Bombardier Beetle

When a Bombardier Beetle is threatened, it squirts burning chemicals from the tip of its abdomen in a series of explosions of heat, color, and noise.

Best Gymnast ● Springtail

A Springtail can jump 40 times its own length to escape predators. As it flies through the air, it does one or more back-somersaults.

Bug Athletes

Best Weight Lifter • Rhinoceros Beetle

A Rhinoceros Beetle, which is as large as a mouse, may be the strongest animal on earth. It can lift about 850 times its own body weight.

World's Smallest Insect • Fairyfly

Fairyflies are tiny, tiny wasps less than .2 mm long, the size of a period at the end of a sentence.

151 When you find a bug of any kind, watch it carefully for a while. Ask yourself, "Could this bug qualify for the Bug Olympics? What event would it compete in?" Make a note in your nature journal. For example, you might write, "The stink bug wins a gold medal for being the stinkiest!"

152 Organize a Bug Olympics. For admission, ask each participant to bring a bug in a jar. Plan events to find the best jumper, flyer, crawler, or runner.

153 Set up an Olympic event for bugs. (You can hold this event with grasshoppers, crickets, millipedes, or caterpillars, as long as every person has the same kind of bug.) Draw a circle about six feet in diameter on the ground with a stick or on a sidewalk with chalk. With some of your friends, catch a bug for each person. Then, one at a time, have a person place his or her bug in the center of the circle and let it go. Use a stopwatch or simply count to see how long it takes the bug to get out of the circle. Whose bug-athlete was the fastest? Did it fly, hop, or crawl?

154 Set up a Free-for-All event. Have each person catch a bug. It doesn't matter what kind of bug it is. Put all of the bugs in the center of your circle at the same time. Watch carefully to see which bug gets out of the circle first and which one is last. Pay attention to the different ways that bugs move and act.

World's Largest Insect • Titan Beetle

The Titan Beetle can reach more than seven inches in length. It can inflict a painful bite, too.

Trickle Creek Books

Bug Lover's Life List

· · · · · · · · · · · · ·

People who are fascinated by a certain kind of animal look for those animals everywhere they go. And they find them! Birders spot birds, butterfly watchers follow butterflies, and bug hunters find bugs. Often people continue their interest in nature throughout their lives. Many people keep a life list — a list of all the animals of a certain kind that they see during their lifetime. Are you ready to begin your Bug Life List today?

Name of Bug	Where found	Date found	Remarks
Dragonfly			
Grasshopper			
Cricket			
Praying Mantis			
Spittlebug			
Leafhopper			
Ladybird Beetle			
Firefly			
Click Beetle			
Butterfly			
Moth			
Caterpillar			
Ant			
Daddy Longlegs			
Millipede			
Pill Bug			
Spider			

Note: You'll want to add more and more pages to your life list as you go along.

Final Activities

155 At first, your life list might be very simple. When you see a caterpillar, you check off "caterpillar" on your list. But as you get better at noticing details, you'll probably want to use a field guide to insects so you can identify them by name. There are wonderful field guides just for kids.

156 Keep a bug scrapbook with field notes, sketches, photos, newspaper and magazine articles, and ideas for bug experiments and observations.

157 Make a bug zoo with some of your friends. Settle each bug in a bug jar with its correct food, water, and shelter. Make a label or a sign for each jar, naming the bug and giving some information about it. Invite other kids and parents to visit your bug zoo.

158 Make a soil zoo for ground beetles, pill bugs, millipedes, slugs, earthworms, etc. by putting a piece of rotting log and soil in a large plastic storage container. Keep it moist. Add decaying leaves and an apple core.

159 Choose one of the activities in this book for a science fair project or design your own experiments with bugs. Begin with a question about the bug, such as "Does this bug like sun or shade?" and then think of a way to answer your question.

160

Remember that bugs are little animals. They are affected by polluted air, water, and soil just as we are. Everything that harms our environment also harms bugs. Some insects are endangered. Some have become extinct. In tropical rainforests, many insects disappear before they can ever be numbered or named. Please do everything you can to protect our earth, so that we can continue to explore and enjoy the wonders of nature — including all of our favorite bugs!

Trickle Creek Books

Glossary: Words for Bug Experts

• • • • • • • • • • •

abdomen - the rear body section of an insect.

anatomy - the study of the form or structure of animals or plants; looking at the different parts of an animal or plant.

antenna (plural: **antennae**) - a pair of slender feelers on the head of an insect.

appendage - a natural, but less important part of a plant or animal, attached to the main part.

aquatic insects - insects that grow or live in water or stay near water.

bug - a term for "creepy crawlies," including insects, spiders, pill bugs, and others. **True bugs** are insects in the group Hemiptera. Almost all true bugs have front wings that fold flat over their backs and beak-like mouth parts.

camouflage - a disguise that enables an insect to hide by looking like part of the environment. A green katydid that looks like a leaf is **camouflaged**.

centipede - *centipede* means "hundred feet."

cerci - a pair of feelers at the rear end of an insect's body.

cheesecloth - a thin cotton cloth with a very loose weave.

clone - a plant or animal that is exactly like another. The daughters of a female aphid are **clones** of its mother.

cocoon - a silken case that an insect larva spins around itself while it goes through the pupa stage of its growth. For example, this is the stage in which a caterpillar changes into a moth.

complete metamorphosis - an insect life cycle in four stages: egg, larva, pupa, and adult.

compound eyes - insect eyes with hundreds, or even thousands, of tiny lenses, giving the insect excellent vision.

chrysalis - a hardened shell in which a butterfly pupa is formed. This is the stage in which a caterpillar changes into a butterfly.

developmental biology - the study of how living things grow and develop.

distress signal - a way that an animal shows it is in trouble or in pain.

diurnal - active in the daytime.

entomologist - a scientist who studies insects.

exoskeleton - a skeleton on the outside of an insect's body.

eyespots - spots on an insect that look like eyes but aren't eyes. **Eyespots** fool or frighten predators.

field guide - a book that helps you identify natural objects, animals, or plants.

frass - insect poop.

gall - an abnormal growth of plant tissue caused by an insect, fungus, or bacteria.

genetics - the study of how animals and plants pass on certain characteristics to their offspring; the science of heredity.

habitat - the place where an animal or plant is normally found.

head - the front body section of an insect, which bears the eyes, antennae, and mouthparts.

hibernate - to spend the winter in a kind of deep sleep.

incomplete metamorphosis - an insect life cycle in only three stages: egg, nymph, and adult.

iridescent - showing many colors that shift and change like colors in a soap bubble.

larva (plural: **larvae**) - the active, feeding stage of an insect that changes to another form when it becomes an adult. Grubs, caterpillars, and maggots are **larvae**.

leaf litter - the fallen leaves, twigs, pine needles, etc. that cover the ground beneath trees and shrubs.

life cycle - a series of stages that an animal passes through during its lifetime.

loupe - a small magnifier.

metamorphosis - a change in form as an insect grows.

migrate - to move from one region to another when the season changes.

millipede - *millipede* means "thousand feet," but no millipede actually has a thousand legs.

mimic - insects that imitate other insects or natural objects in form and color. A praying mantis that looks like a flower is a **mimic**.

mimicry - the ability of an insect to imitate another animal, plant, or natural object.

molt - to shed the old skin as an animal grows.

mouthparts - parts of an insect's mouth used for biting, sucking, piercing, sipping, and lapping.

nocturnal - active at night.

nymph - the immature form of insects before they become adults through incomplete metamorphosis. A young grasshopper, which looks like a little adult, is a **nymph**.

ootheca - the egg case of a praying mantis; it looks like a blob of crisp brownish foam attached to the top or middle of a stem or tall grass. (Many cockroaches also have **ootheceae**.)

overwinter - to last through the winter.

ovipositor - long egg-laying tube found on some female insects. It sticks out from the back of the abdomen.

predator - an animal that attacks and eats other animals.

prey - an animal that is hunted for food by another animal.

pupa (plural: **pupae**) - the resting stage of an insect before it changes into an adult.

rainforest - a tropical forest that receives at least 100 inches of rain each year.

reproduce - to have offspring.

sap - plant juice.

simple eyes - insect eyes that probably see only light and shade.

species - a group of plants or animals that are alike in certain ways and are capable of having offspring.

spinneret - an organ for producing threads of silk. The **spinnerets** of a caterpillar are near its mouth. Those of a spider are at the rear part of its abdomen.

spittle - spit.

spiracles - breathing holes along an insect's body.

terrarium - a glass container in which to grow small plants or to raise tiny animals, including bugs.

thorax - the middle body section of an insect, which bears the legs and wings.

vegetarian - eating no meat, only plants and vegetables.

Trickle Creek Books

Keeping-Bugs Chart

Insect	Food	Water	Shelter	Notes
Ants	Try bits of fruit, cheese, green vegetables, meat, dead insects, bread, honey, and peanut butter. Remove uneaten food each day.	Place a small moist sponge in habitat. Keep it wet every day.	A glass jar with tiny holes punched in lid. Place an unopened soda can inside jar to force ants to tunnel around outside. Fill jar with soil. Wrap jar with black paper. Remove paper to observe ants.	Don't collect ants from more than one colony or they will fight. Try to collect eggs, larvae, and pupae, too.
Caterpillars	Find the exact plant that your caterpillar eats. Provide fresh leaves on stems twice a day. Caterpillars can't eat wilted or dry leaves.	Sprinkle the leaves with water.	Small terrarium with lid or large jar covered with netting. Put soil in the bottom with tiny branches and piece of bark.	Don't let the inside of the container get too wet or too dry. You may have to remove droppings.
Cicadas	Adults don't eat but may suck sap from leaves.	Damp paper towel.	Gallon jar with dirt in bottom. Provide sturdy sticks to climb on.	
Click Beetles	Fresh leaves and flowers (pollen and nectar), although beetles may not eat at all.	Damp paper towel.	Small terrarium with screened lid.	Gather leaves from plant nearest place where beetle was found. Keep leaves on twigs and in container of water, so they stay fresh.
Crickets	Lettuce, bran, dry cat food, raw vegetable scraps.	Droplets from spray bottle. Water in lettuce.	Terrarium or large jar with lid. Add 2 inches of sand and a container of wet sand for egg laying. Add things to hide in like sections of toilet paper rolls.	Spray sand provided for nesting to keep it damp. Use a 60-watt bulb near terrarium to keep temperature warm. Keep away from direct sunlight.
Daddy Longlegs	Bits of juicy fruits and vegetables, dead moths or other insects, oatmeal, nuts, worms, almost anything.	Damp paper towel.	Terrarium with leaf litter.	
Dragonfly Nymphs	May eat nonliving food (raw meat), worms, tadpoles, tiny fish, aquatic insects.	Water from pond or stream where nymph was collected. Keep water shallow (only about 3 inches deep) in aquarium.	Aquarium or large jar with small amount of pond leaf litter on bottom. Provide reed or long stem extending above water.	*Nymphs can bite!* Keep nymph by itself. These predators will eat other creatures in aquarium, even other nymphs.
Fruit Flies	Mixture of over-ripe banana, a little water, and a sprinkling of yeast. Or buy dried banana flakes (which won't mold) from a biological supply company. Mix flakes with water and yeast.	If banana mixture dries, add a little water or cover mouth of jar with wet fabric.	Quart jar with banana mixture in bottom. Cover jar with fabric, secure with a rubber band.	Fruit flies don't buzz, bite, or carry germs. Once they are in jar with banana mix, they need no care.
Grasshoppers	Grasses and plants. Leafy vegetables: lettuce, celery, spinach, cabbage.	Droplets from spray bottle.	7"-x-12" terrarium. Add a few inches of dirt and provide leafy branches to climb on.	

Insect	Food	Water	Shelter	Notes
Ladybird Beetles	Raisins opened and softened in water. Live aphids.	Damp paper towel.	Small cage or jar with a few leaves.	
Millipedes	Decaying plant matter, such as an old apple core or rotting leaves.	Mist their home everyday.	Container with a tight lid. Put t`wo inches of soil in the bottom, then a layer of leaf litter, including oak leaves if possible.	Provide a tiny pile of rocks or a rounded piece of bark so millipedes can hide.
Pill Bugs	Decaying leaf litter, mushrooms, fish food flakes, small slice of apple or potato.	Always keep moist paper towel in cage. Mist often, but not so much that mold appears.	Terrarium or plastic container with lid that has small holes. Add 2 inches damp soil, leaf litter, damp piece of rotting log or bark.	Pill bugs will die if they dry out. Keep their home damp, but watch for mold. Remove uneaten or moldy food quickly.
Praying Mantis Babies from Eggcase	Fruit fly larvae, fruit flies, aphids. Every day, drop one fly for each mantis into terrarium.	Droplets from spray bottle.	Terrarium or large jar with lid.	Keep nymphs together for a while, but then separate them into small groups or they will eat each other.
Praying Mantises	Live crickets and grasshoppers. Offer bits of raw hamburger with tweezers.	Droplets from spray bottle.	A roomy terrarium with a mesh lid. Add a sturdy twig but nothing on the bottom of the terrarium. No sand, dirt, or leaves.	
Spittlebug Nymphs	Leaves and stems of a juicy plant, plant sap.	Plant sap provides water.	No cage needed. Transplant the plant upon which bugs are found into a pot. The nymphs will stay on the plant.	To care for the spittlebug nymphs, you must care for their plant. Water it and give it light.
Whirligig Beetles	Water insects, dead insects, a sliver of cooked meat hung at the surface.		A good-sized aquarium (10" x 20"). Prop a twig so that beetles can climb out of water.	Whirligigs can fly. Keep a fine-mesh lid on the aquarium. Don't put whirligigs with fish!

Remember that bugs are little animals

● ● ● ● ● ● ● ● ● ●

If you want to keep bugs as pets for a while, you must give them the right water, food, and shelter.

● ● ● ● ●

Note: *Bugs in the green rows in the chart can be kept together in one terrarium. Bugs in the blue rows can be kept together too.*

65

Bug Resources

Bugscope

Bugscope is a free project sponsored by the University of Illinois. It allows students anywhere in the world to explore the microscopic world of insects. Kids propose experiments, explore insect specimens at high-magnification, and discuss what they see with scientists – all from a regular web browser. ● http://bugscope.beckman.uiuc.edu

Bug Books

1000 Facts on Bugs edited by Barbara Taylor; Barnes & Noble, 2006.

Beetles by Elaine Pascoe; Blackbirch Press.

Busy with Bugs by Toni Albert; Trickle Creek Books, 2010.

Extreme Bugs by Leslie Mertz; Collins, 2007.

More Pet Bugs: A Kid's Guide to Catching & Keeping Insects & Other Small Creatures by Sally Kneidel; John Wiley & Sons, Inc., 1999.

National Audubon Society First Field Guide: Insects by Christina Wilsdon; Scholastic Inc.

Secret Worlds: Bugs: A Close-Up View of the Insect World by Chris Maynard; Dorling Kindersley, 2001.

Smithsonian Bug Hunter by David Burnie; Dorling Kindersley, 2005.

Spiders and Their Web Sites by Margery Facklam; Little, Brown and Company, 2001.

Super-Size Bugs by Andrew Davies; Sterling, 2008.

The Awesome Book of Bugs by Clizia Gussoni; Running Press Kids, 2008.

Weaving Wonders: Spiders in Your Backyard by Nancy Loewen; Picture Window Books.

Bug Songs

Insects and Spiders, Twin Sisters Science Series.

Songs About Insects, Bugs & Squiggly Things, Kimbo Educational, 2000.

Bugs on Screen

Bugs! (originally released in IMAX theaters), Terminix, 2003.

Eyewitness Insect, Dorling Kindersley Vision, 1994.

Garden Insects by Chris Korrow, Breathe Deep Productions, 2007.

Bug Posters

Letters and numbers photographed on the wings of butterflies. Butterfly Alphabet, Box 39138, Washington, DC 20016 ● www.butterflyalphabet.com

Bug and — Spider Web Sites

bugbios: Shameless promotion of insect appreciation ● www.insects.org

The Entomological Foundation: Committed to building a future for entomology by educating young people about science through insects ● www.entfdn.org

BugGuide.Net!: An online community of naturalists who enjoy learning about and sharing observations of bugs ● http://bugguide.net

CentralPets.Com: Pet care for animals, including bugs, that are kept in captivity • http://www.centralpets.com

Critter Corner: Environmental Education for Kids! • www.dnr.state.wi.us/org/caer/ce/eek/critter/insect/index.htm

The Dragonfly Museum: Photos and information from the Texas A&M Research and Extension Center • http://stephenville.tanu.edu

Entomology Science Education: The greatest show on earth! • http://entscied.cas.psu.edu

Monarch Watch: Monarch butterfly education, conservation, and research • http://monarchwatch.org

Smithsonian National Museum of Natural History, a virtual tour of O. Orkin Insect Zoo • http://www.mnh.si.edu/museum/virtualtour/tour/second/insectzoo/index.html

Songs of Insects: Listen to an online guide to insect songs • www.musicofnature.com/songsofinsects/index.html

The Butterfly WebSite: Extensive list of butterfly exhibits plus photos, videos, and stories • http://butterflywebsite.com

Yahoo! Kids: Find help identifying insects • http://kids.yahoo.com/animals/insects

• • • • • • • • • • • •

Places to Visit Bugs

Audubon Insectarium
423 Canal Street
New Orleans, LA 70178
504-581-4629 • www.auduboninstitute.org

World of Insects Exhibit, Cincinnati Zoo
3400 Vine Street
Cincinnati, OH 45220
513-961-1870 • www.cincinnatizoo.org

There are many more. You'll find bugs at an exhibit in your state.

• • • • • • • • • • • •

Products for Bug Watchers

Buzzerks: Toy glasses with prismatic lenses that roughly mimic a bug's-eye view. Eyeglass frames come in three styles – fire ant, hornet, or mantis. Available from Insect Lore. (See address under Biological Suppliers.)

Garden Spider Web Frame invites a spider to spin a web, Magic Cabin • www.magiccabin.com

Giant inflatable insects, Learning Resources • www.learningresources.com

Larger-than-Life Insect Puzzles: 3-D bug puzzles with 20 to 30 pieces each, realistic details, Mind Ware • www.mindwareonline.com

PopUp Port a Bug, an airy mesh habitat with handy tote, Insect Lore • www.insectlore.com

• • • • • • • • • • • •

Biological Suppliers (where you can buy bugs and equipment)

BioQuip Products, Inc.
2321 Gladwick Street
Rancho Dominguez, CA 90220
310-667-8800 • www.bioquip.com

Carolina Biological Supply Company
2700 York Road
Burlington, NC 27215
800-584-0381 • www.carolina.com

Insect Lore
PO Box 1535
Shafter, CA 93263-1535
800-LIVE BUG • www.insectlore.com

Planet Natural (Praying mantis egg cases)
1612 Gold Avenue, PO Box 3146
Bozerman, MT 59772
800-289-6656 • www.planetnatural.com

Index

glow stick 9
glowworms 33
grasshoppers 8,14,16, 20–21, 59
   air sacs 12
   antennae 21
   camouflage 16
   Field event 21, 59
   gut 12
   heart 12
   how to keep 10, 21
   long-horned 21
   nerve cord 12
   ovaries 12
   salivary glands 12
   short-horned 20–21
   song 57

H
habitat 8, 10
   ant 45
   butterfly 41
   pill bug 53
head 12–13
   praying mantis 25
Hissing Cockroach 56

I
insects 7-8, 12-16, 25, 27, 29,
   35, 37, 45, 49, 53, 55, 56-
   57, 61
insect net 9, 29

J
jar 10–11, 13
   for ants 45
   for fireflies 33
   for fruit flies 47
   for whirligig beetles 37

K
katydid 16
   camouflage 16
   song 56
keeping bugs 10–11

L
ladybird beetles - See ladybugs.
ladybugs 30–31
   eggs 31
   how to keep 10, 31
   larvae 31
larva (larvae) 14–15
   ant 45, 58
   butterfly 38, 40
   firefly 33
   fruit fly 46–47
   ladybug 31
   moth 38, 40
leafhoppers 28–29
   (not) keeping 29
legs 12–13, 15
   caterpillar 38
   centipede 51
   click beetle 35
   daddy longlegs 48–49

leafhopper 28
   grasshopper 12, 20–21
   millipede 50–51
   pill bug 52–53
   praying mantis 24–25
   spider 54
life cycle 10
   butterfly and moth 41
   fruit fly 47
light organs, click beetle 35
luciferin 33

M
magnifying lens 13, 23, 31, 45, 47
metamorphosis 14–15
   complete metamorphosis 14, 40
   incomplete metamorphosis 14
millipedes 8, 13, 50–51, 59
   Fire Millipede 51
   Giant Banded Millipede 51
   how to keep 10, 51
   Pill Millipede 51
mimicry 16
   caterpillar 16
   firefly 33
   praying mantis 16
   treehopper 16
   wasp moth 16
molting 14–15
   cicada nymph 27
   dragonfly nymph 19
   millipede 51
moths 14,16–17, 37, 42–43
   Death's Head Hawk Moth 56
   larva (caterpillar) 38
   pupa (cocoon) 40
   wasp moth 16
mouthparts 12–13

N
nymphs 14
   cicada 27
   dragonfly; damselfly 19
   spittlebug 29

O
ootheca 25
overwinter, ladybugs 30
ovipositor 12
   cricket 23, 57

P
pill bugs 8, 13, 52–53
   how to keep 10, 53
praying mantis 12, 14, 16, 24–25, 53
   camouflage 16
   egg case (ootheca) 25
   flower mantis 16, 25
   forelegs 25
   how to hatch 25
   males and females 25
   mimicry 16, 25
predator 16, 19, 25, 33, 35, 49, 55
prey 19, 25
pupa (pupae) 11, 14

ant 45
   butterfly and moth 40–41
   fruit fly 47

R
rainforest 17, 61
   Army Ants 45
   leafhoppers 29
   Queen Alexandra's Bird-
      wing Butterfly 43

S
scent glands, daddy longlegs 49
simple eyes 12
slugs 8, 49
snails 8, 49
sowbugs 53
space shuttle; space station 47
spiders 8, 13, 49, 54–55
   Black Widow 55
   Brown Recluse 55
   cellar spider 49
   fangs 54
   spinnerets 55
   Wolf Spider 51
spider webs 54–55
   how to collect 55
   kinds of webs 54–55
spiracles 12
spittlebugs 28–29
   how to keep 29
   nymphs 29
Springtail 58

T
terrarium 10–11
   for caterpillars 41
   for click beetles 35
   for crickets 23
   for daddy longlegs 10, 49
   for grasshoppers 21
   for millipedes 10
   for pill bugs 10, 53
thorax 12–13
   caterpillar 38
   click beetle 35
true bugs 7, 14

W
walkingstick, camouflage 16
wasps 14–16
whirligig beetles 36–37
   compound eyes 37
   how to keep 10, 37
wings 12–13
   butterfly 17, 42
   cicada 26–27
   cricket 56
   damselfly 19
   dragonfly 18–19
   firefly 32
   froghopper 29
   fruit fly 46
   grasshopper 12, 20
   leafhopper 29
   praying mantis 25

Author's Note to Parents and Teachers

· · · · · · · · · · · · · · ·

When a child looks at a bug, *really* looks at a bug, becomes still and stares at a bug, that child is opening a door to the nature of science. Collecting bugs introduces children to concepts of habitat and adaptation and diversity. Keeping bugs leads to careful observation, meticulous record keeping, asking questions and making predictions, and finding answers. Getting to know an interesting little animal teaches children about anatomy, life cycles, and patterns of animal behavior. In no time, young bug watchers are doing scientific inquiry and making up their own investigations and experiments.

A child's interest in bugs can easily become the best kind of exploratory learning, driven by curiosity and the desire to know more. Children have many questions, such as, "Do fireflies glow so they can see in the dark?" or "What makes a click beetle click?" Their questions can be springboards that toss them into the study of science. And along the way, they can learn to be kind and respectful to even the smallest of animals, which ultimates in a deep concern for all life on earth.

Thank you for joining me in "teaching kids to care for the earth."

Toni Albert
Trickle Creek

· · · · · · · · · · · · · ·

About the Author and Illustrator

Toni Albert, M.Ed., is an award-winning author of forty-one books. Many of her books are about endangered wildlife and endangered wildlands and reflect her deep concern for the environment. She is the owner of Trickle Creek Books, which is committed to "teaching kids to care for the earth."

Ms. Albert is a lifelong bug watcher who stops in her tracks to study an interesting insect. From childhood, she has single-handedly rescued and released uncounted insects and spiders that strayed indoors.

The author lives on twenty acres of Pennsylvania woodland with her husband Bob, Charlie the cat, and Cooper, a Jack Russell/beagle who looks like a brown and white fox.

Margaret Brandt, M.F.A., has produced award-winning illustrations for the past 29 years. Her work has appeared nationally and internationally on candy wrappers, billboards, advertisements, magazines, and books. This is her sixth children's book with Trickle Creek Books. The illustrations required extensive research into the fantastic world of bugs: "I am awed by the infinite diversity, beauty, and uniqueness of these creatures—and the important part they play in the world."

When Ms. Brandt is not hard at work illustrating, or teaching college students, she gains inspiration from nature by gardening, camping, and running with her team of sled dogs. She lives in Harrisburg, Pennsylvania, with her husband and seven pampered huskies.

71

Other Books by Toni Albert

"Teaching Kids to Care for the Earth"

EcoJournals: With Nature Activities for Exploring the Seasons invite kids to explore the seasons with unusual and exciting nature activities and then to write about their experiences. *A Kid's Spring EcoJournal, A Kid's Summer EcoJournal, A Kid's Fall EcoJournal, A Kid's Winter EcoJournal* Grades 3-up ● 56 pages ● $9.95 each

I Heard the Willow Weep is a primer on the state of the environment. Practical, informative, and project-packed, it provides a unique resource for teaching kids how to care for our earth. *I Heard the Willow Weep* Grades K-5 ● 32 pages ● $15.95 hardcover ● $7.95 paperback

Saving the Rain Forest With Cammie and Cooper Can seven-year-old Cammie and her little brother Cooper find a way to save the rain forests? Yes, they can — with the help of a handsome, talkative parrot called Sunflower. *Saving the Rain Forest With Cammie and Cooper* Ages 2-7 ● 32 pages ● $16.95 hardcover ● $7.95 paperback

The Remarkable Rainforest and *The Incredible Coral Reef* teach kids about two of the most threatened ecosystems on earth. The books include the author's journals and are packed with hands-on activities

Winner of a Teacher's Choice Award and a Parent's Choice Approval

The Remarkable Rainforest Grades 3-8 ● 64 pages ● $10.95

The Incredible Coral Reef Grades 3-8 ● 64 pages ● $10.95

Books by Toni Albert are available from your local bookstore. If your bookstore doesn't have the book you want, ask the bookseller to order it for you. Or you can order from Amazon.com or directly from the publisher:

Trickle Creek Books
800-353-2791 - www.TrickleCreekBooks.com